THE LAST BEST HOPE

Also by Joe Scarborough

Rome Wasn't Burnt in a Day

THE LAST
BEST HOPE

RESTORING CONSERVATISM
AND
AMERICA'S PROMISE

JOE SCARBOROUGH

CROWN
FORUM
NEW YORK

Library of Congress Cataloging-in-Publication Data is available upon request.

ISBN 978-0-307-46369-2

Printed in the United States of America

Design by Level C

10 9 8 7 6 5 4 3 2 1

First Edition

To conservatives of all parties

Contents

THE LAST BEST HOPE

Introduction: The Way Back

By the second year of his presidency, Abraham Lincoln should have been a demoralized man.

Lincoln's military command had stumbled badly through the opening stages of the Civil War. By 1862, the embattled president faced defiance from his generals, failure from his armies, and humiliation across the globe.

By spring, France and Britain were on the verge of recognizing the Confederacy. By summer, Robert E. Lee was chasing Union forces across the Potomac. The president's army would be forced to make a hasty retreat to prepare for the defense of the nation's capital.

But at the end of that terrible year, Abraham Lincoln delivered a message to Congress that was as defiant as it was determined.

On December 1, 1862, that great man told Congress that history left them no choice but to preserve the American Union as the last best hope on earth.

"The dogmas of the quiet past are inadequate to the stormy present," Abraham Lincoln said. "The occasion is piled high with difficulty, and we must rise with the occasion. As our case is new, so we must think anew and act anew. We must disenthrall ourselves, and then we shall save our country."

As it was in Lincoln's time, so it is in ours.

American leaders do not face a nation divided by war or shamed by the institution of slavery. But as with every generation since 1776, we have no choice but to face the difficult occasion that is piled high before us and rise to that challenge.

Our leaders cannot escape history any more than they can ensure our future unless they begin again to think anew.

It is especially critical at this chapter in our nation's history for conservatives to set aside the dogmas of the quiet past and instead explain their vision to a new generation.

This book will lay out that vision.

Our challenges are great, but they can be met by men and women of good faith who are guided by restraint and prudence instead of rabid, unyielding ideologies.

It is time again for conservatives to lead America into the future. But before we figure out how to do that, let's first talk about how conservatism has been defined throughout our history.

As we begin, let me ask you to set aside everything Americans think they know about what it means to be conservative.

Forget that conservatives are now associated with military expansion, Wall Street recklessness, and ideological conformity.

Instead, try to imagine that conservatism is not a political movement at all, but rather a guiding set of principles grounded in reality and restraint, and flexible enough to sustain America through the next century. Moving forward, we must embrace our first principles so that we can revive what Russell Kirk once called "the forgotten genius of conservatism."

British statesman Edmund Burke, the movement's founder, gained international attention 200 years ago with his stinging critique of the French Revolution.

Burke and his followers championed customs and conventions that promoted social stability across the ages while declaring intellectual war against dogmas of all designs. It was, after all, rabid ideologues who very nearly torched Notre Dame and destroyed French civilization.

Mr. Kirk summed up Burke's distrust of dogma in his classic *The Conservative Mind.*

"A terrestrial paradise cannot be contrived by metaphysical enthusiasts; yet an earthly hell can be arranged readily enough by ideologues of one stamp or another."

William Buckley's biographer, Sam Tanenhaus, believes that Burke would be shocked by modern conservatism. After all, the movement's founder had a belief system that was not based on ideological guidelines but rather on his contempt for all ideologies.

Conservatives, for the better part of the last 200 years, followed Burke's lead by shunning rigid dogma and instead attaching themselves to reality, restraint, custom, and convention.

But that approach is a far cry from where Republicans have ventured over the last generation.

ANSWERING RADICALISM WITH RADICALISM

For a quarter-century, we conservatives have allowed ourselves to be defined too easily as rigid ideologues, blindly faithful to an unyielding agenda.

As a member of the 1994 Republican revolution, I plead guilty as charged.

When conservatives stormed Capitol Hill that year, we sought nothing less than the dramatic transformation of Washington and America. We believed that the radicalism of the 1960s needed to be counterbalanced by radicalism from the right.

I remember feeling elated as incoming GOP congressmen delivered one speech after another that endorsed "radical change." We would seek nothing less than the destruction of the 1960s ethos and the man who most embodied that decade: Bill Clinton.

Our drive for change led to a balanced budget, welfare reform, and the remaking of Congress as a political institution.

But the way we fought those political battles also resulted in a government shutdown, bitter partisanship, and the impeachment of a president.

More frustrating was the fact that our perceived extremism also helped reelect in 1996 the same President we ran against two years earlier. We had saved Bill Clinton from political death by coming across as radical to swing voters and making him again appear to be a moderating force in American politics.

We had answered radicalism with radicalism, and the costs were high.

Conservatives lost their bearings again after September 11. President Bush's disciplined response in Afghanistan devolved over time into a foreign policy approach that guaranteed the U.S. military alone would end tyranny across the world.

The Republican president's second inaugural address contained utopian pronouncements so grand that they would have made Woodrow Wilson skittish.

Once again, politicians who described themselves as conservatives answered radicalism with rigid dogma. And once again, the victories gained came at a terrible cost.

My conclusions shouldn't be seen as a criticism of George W. Bush, but rather a reminder to us all. Besides, it would be disingenuous to suggest that I had been anything other than the most conservative of conservatives over the past 15 years.

While in Congress, I

- supported the government shutdown

- criticized Newt Gingrich for not being *conservative enough* on spending and taxes

- had 100 percent ratings with the NRA and pro-life groups

- voted to impeach Bill Clinton twice

- worked tirelessly for George W. Bush during the 2000 Florida recount

- supported the war in Afghanistan

- supported the war in Iraq

- campaigned for George W. Bush's reelection in 2004

LESS GOVERNMENT, MORE CONSISTENCY

I was, to paraphrase Saint Paul, a conservative's conservative. And I still believe that Republican politicians usually lose elections, not because they are too conservative, but because they stray too far from William Buckley's worldview.

But in this book, I will tell you some ways I believe our conservative approach needs to be modified and enlarged. None of those changes discussed here involve a rethinking of the relationship between the individual and the government. That is the essential relationship we have to get right in our republic if it's to work, and one that must again be our primary focus.

I start this book where I began 15 years ago in Congress: I am a conservative of libertarian tilt, and I want the federal government out of our pocketbooks and out of our bedrooms.

That last demand may be difficult for some of my friends to hear. I'll share my thoughts on that subject later, but I will note here that we conservatives can no longer champion federalism in one area and dismiss it in another.

Either we follow the founding fathers' wisdom contained in the Tenth Amendment and honor the Constitution's meaning, or we do not. That means if the Iowa Supreme Court overturns the popular will of the people by nullifying a gay marriage ban, conservatives should respect Iowa's constitutional right to settle the matter and keep the federal government out of the state's business.

We cannot claim the constitutional high ground in our efforts to fight the nationalization of health care and finance while demanding that Washington become entangled in gay marriage debates and ob-gyn issues.

Either we are for a limited federal government, or we are not.

You will also discover in this book that like Bill Buckley I have a lot of Burke in me, and Burke's thinking starts with this: Respect reality. Understand the age you're living in, understand its facts.

Because of Burke—and the words of Russell Kirk and Ronald Reagan—you'll also discover another area where I believe conservatives can make great gains, and that's the environment.

To my friends on the Right I say, "Hear me out. It's the job of conservatives to conserve."

And moving forward, conservatives must be seen as defenders of the environment, American tax dollars, military force, and the historic relationship between the individual and the federal government.

In his conservative classic *Up from Liberalism*, Mr. Buckley wrote,

I will not cede more power to the state. I will not willingly cede more power to anyone, not to the state, not to General Motors, not to the CIA. I will hoard my power like a miser, resisting every effort to drain it away from me. I will then use my power, as I see fit. I mean to live my life an obedient man, but obedient to God, subservient to the wisdom of my ancestors; never to the authority of political truths arrived at yesterday at the voting booth. That is a program of sorts, is it not? It is certainly program enough to keep conservatives busy, and the liberals at bay. And the nation free.

A PRAGMATIC CONSERVATISM

Even the defiant young *National Review* founder understood that standing athwart history and yelling "Stop!" would leave him standing alone more often than not. Still, Buckley's declaration of independence from the ever-expanding state continued to serve throughout his life as a guiding light rather than a rigid ideology.

When California governor Ronald Reagan was attacked by small-government conservatives for betraying their cause, Bill Buckley struck back in a November 1967 *National Review* column. As Tanenhaus noted, Buckley mocked Reagan's critics by asking whether the California governor should "padlock the state treasury and give speeches on the Liberty Amendment."

Buckley praised Reagan in that 1967 column for being pragmatic, and suggested the former movie actor would one day play a great role in American history.

Almost 40 years later, Buckley would still be channeling Burke and Reagan by telling the *Wall Street Journal*, "Conservatism implies a certain submission to reality."

George W. Bush's refusal to recognize that reality in his utopian foreign policy led Buckley to conclude in that same *Wall Street Journal* interview that Mr. Bush was no conservative.

The conservative pragmatism of which Mr. Buckley spoke and Mr. Reagan practiced will serve conservative leaders well in these dark days when our movement represents a "dispossessed and forlorn orthodoxy."

Reagan and Buckley also understood that being conservative was merely a means to the end of strengthening U.S. society by fighting for individual rights and against collectivist agendas. Despite their canonizations by the American Right, neither of these political giants could be confused for what passed as a conservative during the Bush era.

That age, and the one through which we are passing now, should be troubling for conservatives of all parties.

FROM ONE FORM OF RADICALISM TO ANOTHER

America is racing down a radical course whose ending is uncertain at best. We continue in our attempts to brace against the vertiginous changes that have flown past our eyes over the last two decades; but our efforts are in vain.

President Barack Obama's government continues to spend money at a quickening pace.

America's indebtedness to China grows by the day.

European leaders blast Obama's fiscal recklessness as the "road to hell."

The French now lecture us on economic restraint.

Washington's most centered columnist, David Broder, predicts doom as a result of Democratic irresponsibility on entitlement spending.

The Congressional Budget Office projects a crippling economic impact from Mr. Obama's budget schemes.

And even Michael Kinsley admits that Barack Obama and Nancy Pelosi's economic policies could push inflation to 20 percent and cause the United States to default on its debts.

The resulting panic from that bankruptcy could make the Great Depression seem mild by comparison.

Against this grim economic backdrop, the United States finds itself mired in two hot wars that have both lasted longer than World War II.

Our troops are nailed down in over 100 foreign countries. America's top generals warn that their armies are at a breaking point. And the United States remains the de facto 9-1-1 to the world.

Historian Paul Kennedy, who wrote the foreign policy classic

The Rise and Fall of the Great Powers, may have been prescient when he warned of America's coming collapse as a global empire.

Kennedy, who compared U.S. military expansion to the policies of past empires, has long been scorned by conservatives as unduly pessimistic. But the historian may be remembered as a prophet if Washington politicians do not wake up soon.

Meanwhile, socialists of all parties remain so ideologically intransigent that they refuse to face up to the most stubborn of facts: America's entitlement system cannot withstand the oncoming crush of baby boomers.

Social Security, Medicare, and Medicaid will collapse and drag the U.S. economy down with them unless conservative reform is enacted soon.

That is not a matter of opinion; that is a matter of math.

HELPING MAIN STREET, TAMING WALL STREET

Another area of American life that should be wrenching to classical conservatives is the radical transformation of the U.S. economy engineered by Wall Street over the past quarter-century.

For those conservatives who have long believed that Washington's proper role is to preserve a stable society and moral order, the long list of panics that have rocked our financial sector since 1987 should be as disturbing as any development they have witnessed in decades.

Politicians in both parties have failed miserably to restore order to a system buffeted by technological changes that allowed Wall Street titans to create booms and busts with blinding speed.

Never before has the U.S. markets endured so many financial bubbles. And never before have we faced a greater need to restore order and confidence to our markets.

Conservatives must continue to fight against the overregulation of small businesses, but must also understand that it can never again adopt a laissez-faire attitude toward Wall Street.

Failing to properly regulate a system so prone to chaos is anything but conservative.

From Black Monday in 1987 to the Asian crisis of 1997, to the Long-Term Capital Management debacle of 1998, to the Internet collapse of 2000, to the Enron scandal of 2001, to the telecom crash of 2002, to the mortgage meltdown of 2008, Wall Street wizards have been let loose in U.S. markets to live large on leverage and speculation.

Americans eventually followed suit by turning their homes into gigantic credit cards. The United States of America got fat off of easy credit and cheap dollars. Vulgar consumerism became the order of the day. Savings rates dropped to zero.

Shopping in malls became a pastime. And few Americans, *including myself*, were immune from the allure of spending beyond our means. It was if we took to heart the words of John Maynard Keynes, who flippantly dismissed long-term concerns about his economic programs by simply saying, "In the long run we're all dead."

Now we are.

These are not the observations of a reactionary longing for simpler days. I am no more nostalgic for the past than I am fearful of the future.

I still believe America's greatest chapter has yet to be written.

How can I be optimistic in such troubling times? Maybe it is because the American people have proven time and time again to possess remarkable regenerative skills.

Over the past century, the citizens of our great land have absorbed the shock of two world wars, a global flu epidemic that killed more U.S. citizens than World War II, a Great Depression, eleven recessions, the upheavals of the 1960s, Vietnam, Watergate, impeachment, a contested presidential election, and the attacks of September 11.

During that same century, the United States triumphed over the twin scourges of Nazism and Communism.

While American cities were burning, our country was following through on John Kennedy's promise to send a man to the moon. And the same global critics who have continuously castigated the United States as a racist culture watched Americans do what no other majority-white country has done: elect a black man as their president.

The United States of America has endured challenges much greater than the economic one it faces now. But sadly, our greatest burden ahead may be the shortsightedness of our own leaders.

TWO PARTIES WITH FEW DIFFERENCES

Throughout the first decade of the twenty-first century, Washington politicians have been behaving as recklessly as the Wall Street schemers they currently condemn.

Republicans under George W. Bush took a $150 billion surplus and turned it into a $1 trillion deficit. The GOP also doubled the national debt, presided over a staggering trade deficit, allowed the dollar to collapse, passed massive tax cuts, burdened a crippled entitlement system with $7 trillion in new debt, and allowed domestic spending to grow at its fastest rate since the Great Society.

William Buckley was once again proven right: George W. Bush was not a conservative.

Despite my personal affection for the man, the sad truth is that President Bush spent America into debt, tore apart its conservative movement, and left his own political party shattered.

Americans punished the GOP for his dreadful performance

with landslide defeats in 2006 and 2008. Democrats, led by a char-
ismatic candidate of change, were granted a monopoly of power in
Washington.

But sadly, America's crisis went from bad to worse.

In its cover story "We Are All Socialists Now," *Newsweek*
identified the central paradox of the sweeping economic plan
Barack Obama passed through Congress in the early months of
his administration.

Mr. Obama chose to respond to a crisis brought on by too much
spending and too much debt with even more spending and even
more debt. Few others in the national press noted the absurdity of
the president trying to get out of debt by racking up historic
deficits.

Because of his history-bending approach to money and math, it
became evident soon after his inauguration that Barack Obama
was not the thoughtful, postpartisan leader he passed himself off
as during the 2008 campaign.

Within two weeks of his uplifting inaugural address, the new
president was pushing a partisan stimulus bill that proposed
spending more money than any legislation in U.S. history.

The same politician who had promised to bring partisans together instead shut down bipartisan debate with the declaration "I
won."

The same White House that quoted scripture to urge politicians
to put aside childish things relied on push polls to target controversial talk-show hosts and then childishly proclaim them to be
leaders of the opposition party.

And the same Barack Obama who promised to put Americans'
interests ahead of his own ambitions chose instead to use the suffering of those same Americans as a device to advance his agenda.

As his chief of staff famously said, "You never want to waste a
good crisis."

Because the Obama White House proved itself so quickly to be adept at using an economic meltdown for political gain, the balance of power between the citizen and state is shifting radically.

The relationship between private enterprise and the central state is changing forever.

And the intellectual friction between individualists and collectivists that has balanced federalism debates since the time of Jefferson and Hamilton has been trampled underfoot.

One week our elected leaders pass a stimulus package that is the largest spending bill in U.S. history. The next our president proposes a budget that approaches $4 trillion.

A $750 billion bank bailout is promised the same week that Barack Obama promotes a $634 billion "down payment" on universal health care.

And despite warnings from the Congressional Budget Office, Mr. Obama and Ms. Pelosi continue to charge forward exploiting a bailout culture left to them by President Bush providing carte blanche to fundamentally alter American society.

It is not hyperbole to suggest that the capitalist system that has made America the world's envy for over 250 years is facing its greatest domestic challenge in the form of Barack Obama.

But what is most disturbing about the Obama revolution is its ad hoc nature.

Inconsistent policy proposals fire out of the White House with stunning speed, as trillion-dollar price tags litter Washington policy meetings.

Millions of Americans who saw their retirement accounts collapse now must watch Treasury Secretary Tim Geithner show himself to be no more effective in crisis communications than former Treasury Secretary Hank Paulson and Federal Reserve chief Ben Bernanke.

OBAMA: THE ONLY THING WE HAVE TO FEAR IS . . . EVERYTHING!!!

President Obama has been equally ineffective in reassuring Main Street.

In fact, the new president immediately made matters worse by fanning the flames of fear. The president spent his first few months in the White House making regular predictions about America's bleak future.

He went so far as to ominously warn that Republicans' failure to pass his political programs could prevent the United States of America from *ever* recovering from the current economic recession.

Mr. Obama's dire warnings became so bleak that Bill Clinton told ABC News that the new president should stop having such a grim outlook on America's economy.

The fact that any president would employ fear as aggressively as Obama in the middle of an economic crisis is surprising. But these fear tactics were being used as political weapons by the same president who had told Americans in his inaugural address a month before that "on this day, we have chosen hope over fear."

But in a few short weeks, the candidate of hope was using raw fear to pass a bloated stimulus package.

Barack Obama may have thought his approach was a new forthrightness in American politics, but there was nothing groundbreaking about his employing Nixonian devices that cynically assumed Americans would always vote their fears over their hopes.

America learned quickly that the White House would not channel FDR's eternal optimism but rather embrace the gloomy outlook of Edgar Allan Poe.

Making matters worse was the fact that the new president spent his first three months avoiding the banking crisis that was central to America's economic challenge.

Instead, President Obama followed his chief of staff's advice and used Americans' suffering to press forward with an expansion of the federal government's reach into the free market that can only be characterized as radical.

Republicans on Capitol Hill have been predictably outraged by the Democratic president's actions.

"Simply raising taxes to cover funding for unnecessary or wasteful programs is not the answer and will only further harm our faltering economy," said the top Republican appropriator Jerry Lewis.

But many protesting GOP leaders were also the same ones who had acted so recklessly during the Bush years. Because of their own dismal record, these GOP bulls seemed like little more than political opportunists striking out at a Democratic president.

It was much of the same on conservative airwaves, where right-wing TV and radio hosts had enabled GOP leaders during the Bush years by their silence. But now they were suddenly shocked by the dangerous debt that was accumulating in Washington.

When I wrote a 2004 book predicting that continued irresponsible spending would destroy the Republican majority and wreck the U.S. economy, conservative leaders considered me a traitor to their cause.

Even though my predictions were proven correct, I could not have foreseen the extent of the damage.

The $7.5 trillion national debt I complained about in my hardcover book ballooned to $9 trillion when my paperback came out 18 months later.

The $450 billion yearly deficit I found unfathomable in 2004 will reach $1.5 trillion by the end of this year.

To put those numbers in perspective, Barack Obama's administration will accumulate more debt over the next 12 months than every president from George Washington to Ronald Reagan.

As unbelievable as that may seem, it gets worse.

Mr. Obama's budget will add more debt to the U.S. economy

over the next decade than the total accumulated by the 43 presidents who preceded him.

If that is not a "radical economic policy," what is?

WARNING TO IDEOLOGUES OF ALL PARTIES

Despite my concerns about Barack Obama's policies, I begin this book by issuing the same warning to ideologues I delivered in the introduction to *Rome Wasn't Burnt in a Day*.

The book you are about to read is not a polemic.

I will not waste my time telling you that one political party represents all that is right in Washington, while the other is the embodiment of evil. That cartoonish approach may sell books, but it offers no hope for those who seek a safer course for our country.

I also want to make sure that you understand that while I have great concerns about Mr. Obama's and Mr. Bush's policies, I will not personally attack the 43rd or 44th presidents of our United States.

I respect both men as husbands, fathers, and patriots. Even though I know that both leaders want only the best for our country, it is my personal belief that their policies and actions taken together have placed America on a dangerous path.

And although I don't like criticizing a new president any more than I do one who just left Washington, America has no more time to waste.

Now is the time to take an honest look at how our country has gotten so badly off track and how we conservatives must right its course.

The past decade has taught us that the battle we face is not simply a fight between Democrats and Republicans, but rather a political standoff between Washington and the rest of America.

Despite what you read in the papers and see on TV, most Americans are not shifting to the right or the left politically.

Like Burke and Buckley, they are suspicious of a blind faithfulness to ideology and instead demand that politicians seek commonsense solutions to the problems we face as a country.

As Buckley said in 2005, we conservatives are captive to reality. So are America's voters.

The same people who elected a progressive Democrat in 1992 turned around and elected a conservative Congress two years later. And those pollsters and pundits who keep telling me that Americans are too shortsighted to elect leaders who promise less government always overlook the conservative triumphs of the 1990s.

The press got it wrong when trying to explain why Republicans lost the 2006 and 2008 elections so badly. It was not because they were too conservative; instead, it was because they were too radical—too radical with our money, too radical with the troops, and too radical with their rhetoric.

The United States of America is a conservative country.

Its people are instinctively repelled by ideology of one stripe or another. It was the radicalism of the Left in the 1960s that made Republicans seem like the safe choice in 1968.

In describing that election, Garry Wills wrote in the *National Review,*

The liberal Eastern establishment found that it was not needed on Election Day—which made its leaders take a second look at the forgotten American, at an angry baffled middle class, paying the bill for progress, who found its values mocked by the spokesmen of that progress. These voters felt cheated, disregarded, robbed of respect.

Americans did, in fact, respond to campus radicalism and urban riots by electing Richard M. Nixon. For Middle America, Nixon's promise of social order trumped the Democrats' call for social justice.

America's collapse in Vietnam coupled with the shame of Watergate made the election of a Democratic peanut farmer possible. Eight years later, Nixon had promised to bring stability to America's political system, but instead offered voters only more chaos.

Jimmy Carter promised the return of principled leadership to Washington.

But President Carter's four years were filled with instability, culminating in a humiliating hostage crisis. Worse for Mr. Carter was the fact that the bill for 15 years of government expansion starting with the Great Society came due on his watch.

Throughout the 1980 campaign, Democrats tried to paint Ronald Reagan as an out-of-touch ideologue. But the Left's irresponsible reign made Reagan's landslide inevitable.

Far from being seen as dangerous, the man who told voters that Washington was "the problem" became seen as a moderating force on a runaway welfare state.

For the next three decades, politicians debated issues involving the government's reach on Ronald Reagan's terms. The Republican revolution of 1994 only made Reagan's calls for restraint on reckless government growth echo more loudly through Washington corridors.

The GOP Congress that took control with the 1994 landslide promised to reduce Washington's power and reach. For its efforts, conservative legislators were returned to power in 1996, 1998, 2000, 2002, and 2004.

Like Ronald Reagan, my conservative colleagues and I campaigned to reduce the size and power of Washington bureaucracies.

Unlike President Reagan, we were able to succeed in limiting the explosive growth of government, balancing the budget, reforming welfare, paying down the national debt, saving Medicare, and changing the way Washington worked.

A $300 billion deficit was turned into a $150 billion surplus, and the real power in Congress shifted from older appropriators to younger reformers like myself.

CONSERVATIVES AS A MODERATING FORCE

Once upon a time, conservatives told voters exactly what we would do after getting elected. We then had the temerity to keep our word.

That unique approach worked so well that voters allowed conservatives to control Congress throughout the 1990s. And despite the fact that most in the Washington establishment dismissed us as right-wing fanatics, American voters kept reelecting us because we were seen as a moderating force against those same Beltway elites.

Like Reagan before us, we were called extremists inside the nation's capital but labeled conservatives west of the Potomac.

But that would soon change.

The great ideological overreach by Republicans began in earnest with the arrival of George W. Bush to the White House. The Bush presidency would provide Republicans with a monopoly of power that ultimately proved damaging to the conservative movement and the country as a whole.

Suddenly, the same conservatives who had spent years legislating against Bill Clinton's worst instincts became a rubber stamp for Mr. Bush's.

The GOP administration was allowed to run up massive debts at home and engage in an exhausting foreign policy abroad.

Republican mismanagement of the Iraq War and Hurricane Katrina also destroyed the party's brand by showing its leaders to be no more competent than the hapless Democrats they had long scorned.

Mr. Bush's second inaugural address would further distance the president from American voters and world leaders by promising the use of U.S. military force to democratize all four corners of the globe.

The former Texas governor eventually took on the worst spending traits of Lyndon Johnson at home and the most utopian characteristics of Woodrow Wilson abroad.

The self-described conservative president had suddenly become seen by swing voters as extreme, and his approval rating sank into the 20s. Through his blunders and bloated budgets, Mr. Bush somehow managed to even make San Francisco's Nancy Pelosi seem like a moderating force as speaker for middle Americans.

In 2006, Democrats routed Republicans in House and Senate races. Americans once again voted to counterbalance what they saw as ideological extremism.

Two years later, the sins of GOP leaders coupled with John McCain's erratic response to the banking meltdown made the U.S. Senate's most liberal member seem like the safest presidential pick for millions of Americans. This was true despite the fact that most neutral political observers agreed with *Newsweek*'s assessment that the American electorate was still right of center.

Few voters outside the Republican base seemed to care about Barack Obama's left-wing voting record or his former radical associates. Instead, swing voters cared more about their future than Barack Obama's past. So they once again elected the candidate they believed most capable of advancing social stability and economic order.

EVOLUTION OVER REVOLUTION

Americans are now, and have always been, classically conservative. As President Reagan's first budget director concluded after the "Reagan Revolution" faced resistance, voters do not have a taste for revolutions of any sort.

Americans may grudgingly accept ideological evolutions, but only when that change is necessary to win wars, end recessions, or advance social causes that will further stabilize society. But when those political evolutions transform into ideological revolutions, the partisans leading the charge are usually routed at the ballot box.

The most recent examples of dogma destroying political majorities were the Democrats' defeat in 1968 and the Republicans' collapse in 2008.

As Tom Brokaw's book *Boom* so brilliantly illustrated, a generation of liberals paid for the Left's excesses in the 1960s.

America's center was repelled by the extremism they saw on their TV sets every night, and as Garry Wills explained in the *National Review*, voters took their anger out on the ideologues who were seen as fanning the flames of social unrest.

The question for the next generation of conservative leaders is whether they will allow their movement to face a generation of defeat and disappointment, or whether they will learn instead from the Left's political trail of tears.

If conservatives are to move forward to victory, they must again find the middle of American political life and stop being seen as liberals were for a generation: as a tone-deaf movement littered with self-consumed ideologues.

Getting past that ideological branding will require a change in attitude and a new conservative pragmatism every bit as flexible as William F. Buckley's when defending his friend Ronald Reagan.

Mr. Buckley, like the prophets of old, understood that there was a season for advancing, a season for holding steady, and a season for taking tactical retreats.

Great conservative minds like Buckley's have long recognized that simply reciting dogmata from political texts is not a viable political option, unless one wishes to be beaten at the voting booth with great regularity. Again, true conservatives align themselves with reality and restraint.

The prophets wrote of a natural order to the seasons and how with each season came a time to live, a time to love, a time to build up, and a time to break down. In my own life, I have succeeded when I have been able to recognize the coming of a season when my most prudent course was throwing caution to the wind.

Even during such days, I remained mindful of the dangers that a shifting breeze could bring. When that change occurred, it was time to narrow my focus, lie low, and wait for the oncoming storm.

For America, that storm has already hit.

Too many of us were ill prepared for the changing of seasons, so the altering winds brought traumatic results. In this season we now find ourselves, even the most arrogant Wall Street trader has been humbled.

Perhaps the era of building castles to our most vain conceits has finally come to an end.

THE COMING CONSERVATIVE AGE

The time for restraint is upon us. And ironically, the candidate of change who so ably tapped into America's hopes last year may be the last to feel the seismic shift occurring under him.

In a season of debt, he dreams of spending more.

In a time of restraint, he practices radicalism.

And in an age of prudence, the president embraces rosy economic scenarios.

Barack Obama may soon be a man out of time.

Instead of building empires abroad, Americans will soon expect their leaders to balance their books at home. Personal savings rates will rise, and a new era of responsibility will erase the shabby standards we set for ourselves over the past generation.

Americans will also come to recognize that we neither have the supernatural power nor the political will to single-handedly fulfill George W. Bush's guarantee of a world without tyranny.

Americans will demand that our leaders instead work with a community of nations to provide comfort for those in need. Our elected officials will also have to refuse to engage in military adventurism or the advancement of international social work on the backs of our troops.

Americans will also become impatient with politicians who fail to put our financial house in order. Now is the season to toss aside economic ideologies and begin the warm embrace of simple math.

It may not be sexy, but it sure is safe.

The U.S. government is heading toward bankruptcy and can only be saved by grown-ups who have the courage to tell its citizens that the centralized state has once again promised too much and planned too little.

We must change our ways.

We cannot avert our eyes from this crisis. A glorious war or a mission to Mars will not cause the coming storm to pass. Instead, we must realize like Joseph of Genesis that the season for saving begins today.

Whether you are a Republican or a Democrat, a Libertarian or a Marxist, understand that it is historically inevitable that the "Age of Conservatism" is coming soon.

The winds of history provide us no other choice.

I will try to explain in this book exactly where these historical trends will lead us as a people. But briefly, this new age will mean prudence at home, restraint abroad, and the toning down of political rhetoric that has coarsened our debate for the past generation.

It will also be a time to put aside childish things whether or not the Democratic president chooses to follow his own advice.

We will focus less on how our political enemies have wronged us in the past and concentrate more on how we can lift Americans in the future.

Conservative leaders will also need to take a more prudent path on the environment by declaring war on foreign oil.

It must be our generation that creates a new economy to fuel the globe throughout the next American Century.

As a conservative nation, we will also need to act more responsibly to save Social Security and Medicare. Gone are the days when conservatives can dismiss these programs as illegitimate.

These retirement safety nets have become part of Washington's social contract with its senior citizens, and the continued undermining of these programs by Democrats will only tear apart our country's social order.

We will save Social Security and Medicare despite the fact that Nancy Pelosi's party has shamelessly demagogued the issue for years. But rest assured, Democrats' radicalism on this subject will soon be revealed.

Despite classical conservatives' long-standing distrust of rigid ideologies, I do not believe conservative leaders should seek out a mushy middle ground where frightened politicians cower. Rather, I propose an agenda that is radical only in its restraint, that is subversive only in its prudence.

It does not promise the flowering of democracy across the planet any more than it guarantees the curing of cancer at home.

Instead, conservatives must promote an approach that recognizes the reality that one day soon, the great winds of history will again be at America's back. And if our elected officials become wise enough to first do no harm, the United States of America will once again become that city shining brightly on a hill for all the world to see.

We will again experience the full energy of those gales. We will use that power with the greatest of restraint, and we will again be the last best hope for a dying world.

1 INCREASING MILITARY POWER THROUGH RESTRAINT

AVOIDING AN EARTHLY HELL

> We must be judicious in our use of the military. We will fight only when it is in the vital interests of the United States, when our mission is clear, and when the exit strategy is obvious.
>
> —*Governor George W. Bush*

The morning after George W. Bush made his farewell address to the nation, few media outlets took note of it. In fact, the only national paper to mention the 43rd president's final speech on its front page was *USA Today,* and it confined the story to a small box that described another article hidden inside.

America's newspapers were focused instead that morning on an airplane that had been taken down from the skies over Manhattan.

TV crews dutifully rushed to the crash site and almost immediately began warning Americans of a grave new danger that would threaten the safety of air travelers for years to come.

Tom Costello of NBC News told *Morning Joe* viewers that government officials were working furiously to address the problem and that the crisis had become so grave in the nation's capital that cannons were being fired from the end of Reagan National Airport's runways every three minutes.

The *Times* of London weighed in the next morning with a list of solutions government officials were considering to protect British passengers from this growing menace. The *Times* reported that some leaders had become so desperate that they were resorting to clandestine poisoning, dog attacks, and advanced radar technology.

Coincidentally, a few days earlier the U.S. government had released a report showing that for the first time in aviation history, the United States had gone two years without suffering a single casualty on a commercial air carrier. So just when Americans thought it was safe to once again climb aboard a plane without fear of attack, their confidence was jolted by a rising threat that now stalked the not-so-friendly skies.

We had again met our enemy in the air over New York City, and what was it?

Birds.

As Tom Costello helpfully explained to viewers, the Canada goose population was on the migratory rise and its effect was being felt on runways across America. That phenomenon had ended in the miraculous water landing on the Hudson River of a US Airways flight.

How ironic it must have seemed to the man who saw his presidency defined by four plane crashes within an hour's time that his farewell address to America was eclipsed by yet another plane crash in Manhattan. He must have felt some pride in the fact that the culprits seven years later were not a group of terrorists intent on destroying our way of life, but instead a group of birds trying to avoid a very loud object flying their way.

Predictably, few in the media noted the difference George W. Bush's presidency had made to the safety of Americans from a terrorist attack. And while debates might rage for years to come over his approval of harsh interrogation techniques or how long enemy combatants could be locked up, those battles will be waged in law schools like Columbia and NYU, instead of inside the concourses of LaGuardia or JFK.

George W. Bush had made the protection of American citizens and the prevention of future terror attacks on U.S. soil his top priority. By that measure—the most important many apply to a commander in chief—the 43rd president did what few Americans thought possible in the weeks following September 11.

He kept Americans safe at home.

While President Bush accomplished that task, conservatives now must assess the cost of achieving that goal and determine how America's actions over the past eight years have impacted their movement and, more important, U.S. foreign policy for the next generation.

Before discussing the most effective conservative approach to foreign policy in the future, we should first review how much of a break Mr. Bush's approach was from a conservative foreign policy tradition that was once defined by realism and restraint.

Why did conservative leaders respond to the events of that September morning the way they did?

Why did the same cautious Republicans who resisted Bill Clinton's calls for military intervention in Bosnia, Kosovo, Haiti, Sudan, and Iraq adopt George W. Bush's preemption doctrine without question?

And why did so few conservatives criticize Mr. Bush's Wilsonian pronouncement that the United States of America would lead a global democratic revolution that would end tyranny itself?

What exactly were conservatives thinking during Mr. Bush's second inaugural address when the Republican president promised the world that U.S. troops would single-handedly bring freedom and peace to all corners of the globe?

Why did the same Republicans who quoted Colin Powell's doctrine to justify their restrained foreign policy approach in the 1990s treat General Powell's cautiousness toward Iraq with such contempt in 2002?

And how did a president who promised to conduct a limited, humble foreign policy reside over an administration that critics on both the left and right derided as utopian?

George W. Bush's foreign policy goals in the 2000 presidential campaign were consistent with those of conservatives like myself who were swept into Congress in 1994. When we controlled the Armed Services Committee during the Clinton administration, prudence and restraint were our guiding principles.

Republicans saw Bill Clinton's use of military force as undisciplined and reckless. As one *Foreign Affairs* article at the time stated, the Clinton cabinet seemed to view foreign policy as an extension of social work. We conservatives used our majority in Congress to attack that approach as unfocused, undisciplined, and Wilsonian.

For most conservatives, the Cold War was a necessary evil.

U.S. global involvement was the only option available for the containment of the Communist threat. But after the Soviet Union fell, Republicans I served with in Congress believed that the United States should engage in less military adventurism while narrowing its focus abroad.

So cautious were many conservatives involving the use of military power that Democratic policymakers like President Clinton's secretary of state, Madeleine Albright, accused GOP leaders of standing in the way of humanitarian missions run by military units.

She was right. We did. And we were proud of it.

No conservative I worked with on the Armed Services Committee in Congress was comfortable with President Clinton's eagerness to dispatch troops to Haiti, Somalia, Bosnia, or Kosovo. We were especially troubled with the Balkans crisis, believing that the lessons of Vietnam taught American leaders not to get involved in civil wars where there were no direct U.S. national security interests.

Conservatives repeatedly pressed Clinton administration officials to state what overriding national interest justified the risking of U.S. casualties. The best answer the White House could provide at the time was that not getting involved in the Balkans civil war would damage our reputation within NATO.

That answer was far from sufficient for most Republicans, who feared getting involved in a three-sided civil war. Obviously, those prudent concerns would fade quickly once a Republican was sworn in as commander in chief.

"We are not the world's 9-1-1," GOP lawmakers would regularly admonish Clinton aides who repeatedly ignored our warnings of an overstretched military.

A NARROW FOCUS. A DEADLY AIM.

Conservatives would also use their perch in the majority to lecture Clinton officials on the finer points of what, for some of us, was the Magna Carta of conservative foreign policy: the Weinberger Doctrine.

Named after Reagan's secretary of defense, Caspar Weinberger's approach to foreign wars was clear, concise, and restrictive. It was framed by the bloody disasters of Vietnam and Beirut, in which two truck bombs struck separate buildings that killed hundreds of U.S. Marines.

Secretary Weinberger said American combat troops should only be deployed when:

1. it is vital to U.S. national interests

2. our troop commitment is full and overwhelming

3. the objectives for our troops are clearly defined

4. leaders will be willing to constantly reassess troop levels and end goals of the operation

5. Americans support the war before engagement

6. U.S. combat troops are sent in only as a last resort

Weinberger's guidelines were taken as gospel by many conservatives throughout the 1980s and outlasted his time in office. When troops rolled into Kuwait in 1991 for the First Gulf War, former Weinberger aide Colin Powell was chairman of the Joint Chiefs.

General Powell's statements at the start of those combat operations showed that he had clearly adopted his boss's approach to warfare.

When asked to describe his military strategy against the Iraqi army, the general was blunt.

"First we're going to cut it off, then we're going to kill it."

And that is exactly what Powell's military machine did.

After the Gulf War, General Powell outlined his own guidelines for U.S. troop deployment. Like Weinberger before him, Powell argued that American troops should go to war only as a last resort. But when we did engage militarily, the force applied should be decisive.

"We don't want a fair fight" was Powell's mantra.

While most Republicans cheered the general's approach, a strand within the conservative movement—dubbed "neoconservatives"—sided with liberal humanitarian hawks like Secretary of State Albright, who were more liberal with the use of American troops overseas in the cause of "limited" wars.

General Powell would remain at odds with both groups.

After leaving the White House for the first time in the mid-1990s, Powell recalled one memorable exchange with Albright, who became exasperated with the general's reluctance to send Americans to war.

"What's the point of having this superb military you're always talking about," Albright asked Powell, "if we can't use it?"

Powell remembered later that he "almost had an aneurysm."

After collecting his thoughts, the chairman of the Joint Chiefs patiently explained to the secretary of state that "American GIs are not toy soldiers to be moved around on some sort of global game board."

The *New York Times* later quoted Secretary Albright as saying that her aggressive worldview was shaped by Britain's appeasement of Adolf Hitler at Munich. Because of that experience, when it came to troop deployment, her first instinct was to "go in." But because Colin Powell and the band of brothers he served with in Vietnam continued to carry the scars of that failed war, their first instinct had always been caution.

Exercising prudence in foreign policy was also the instinct of a popular governor from a large Southern state. His view on how America should engage in world affairs was clear and restrictive, and owed much to Colin Powell.

During a presidential debate with Al Gore, Jim Lehrer asked Governor George W. Bush whether the United States should engage in nation building. The Texas governor's response was every bit as indignant as Colin Powell's retort to Secretary Albright.

"Maybe I'm missing something here," Governor Bush shot back at Lehrer, "but we should encourage people who live in those lands to build their own nations." Bush continued, "Our military is meant to fight and win wars. And when it gets overextended, its morale drops."

The 2000 GOP nominee then gave Americans a condensed version of the Weinberger-Powell Doctrine: "We must be judicious in our use of the military. We will fight only when it is in the vital interests of the United States, when our mission is clear, and when the exit strategy is obvious."

It was as clear a description of conservative foreign policy that existed at the turn of the century.

And then came September 11.

A WAR WITHOUT END

In the immediate aftermath of the attacks on New York and Washington, President Bush began mobilizing the nation for war. The first target was Afghanistan, and on October 7, 2001, that country was invaded.

By November, Kabul had fallen under U.S. control and triggered the collapse of the Taliban throughout the country. America had liberated Afghanistan from one of the most sadistic regimes in history, their citizens were cheering in the streets, and it looked as though the war itself would be easy.

By the end of 2001, some conservatives were mocking the *New York Times*'s R. W. Apple for calling the Afghanistan war a quagmire. But nearly a decade later, history may be on the side of Mr. Apple. Afghanistan could be remembered as the "longest war" of the "long war."

Soon after 9/11, George W. Bush made it clear that Afghanistan would not be the U.S. military's only target. In the president's September 20, 2001, address to Congress, Mr. Bush told America the War on Terror would be neither quick nor limited.

"Our War on Terror begins with al Qaeda," he said, "but it does not end there. It will not end until every terrorist group of global reach has been found, stopped, and defeated."

In his 2002 state of the union address, President Bush went further by labeling Iraq, Iran, and North Korea as the "Axis of Evil." Mr. Bush told Americans that those countries were arming themselves to threaten the peace of the world.

"We'll be deliberate," Mr. Bush added, "yet time is not on our side. I will not wait on events while dangers gather. I will not stand by as peril draws closer and closer. The United States of America will not permit the world's most dangerous regimes to threaten us with the world's most destructive weapons."

Iraq was once again in America's gun sights.

"I SAID WHAT?!?"

While many now debate the wisdom of the Iraq War, most policymakers on both sides of the aisle agreed with Mr. Bush's assessment of Saddam Hussein's regime in the months leading up to the 2003 invasion.

It was assumed by virtually everyone who held a position of power in Washington that Saddam had weapons of mass destruction.

As Bill Clinton's own national security adviser told Congress near the end of the Clinton term, the Iraqi tyrant had used WMD repeatedly in the past decade and would use them again.

That assessment was shared by Bill Clinton, Al Gore, John Kerry, Ted Kennedy, Hillary Clinton, Barack Obama, U.S. intelligence agencies, and those of other nations.

Even the Arab world, the United Nations, and the Iraqi leader's own high command believed Saddam possessed WMD.

One of Hussein's closest aides, Tariq Aziz, recalls Saddam Hussein calling his top military leaders together as American troops bore down on Baghdad. Saddam told them that despite what they had been led to believe, there would be no WMD to repel the oncoming U.S. troops.

The Iraqi high command sat in stunned silence as they absorbed Saddam's words.

Beyond the presumed weapons threat, Saddam Hussein was also a genocidal dictator who had killed more Muslims than any ruler in history, had incited two major wars, had used Iraq as a state sponsor of terror, and had defied sixteen UN resolutions since the end of the 1991 Persian Gulf War.

Without September 11, no American leader would have moved against Iraq in 2003.

But one year after the World Trade Center towers were reduced to rubble, the calculus had changed. And though it is not fashionable to bring up such stubborn facts years later, that calculus shifted for Democrats as well as for Republicans.

One of the president's most dramatic shifts in the area of foreign policy was announced on June 1, 2002, when Mr. Bush told a West Point graduating class that their military careers would be shaped by a new doctrine that would focus less on multinational cooperation and more on preemptive strikes carried out by the U.S. unilaterally.

> We cannot defend America and our friends by hoping for the best. We cannot put our faith in the word of tyrants, who solemnly sign nonproliferation treaties and then systematically break them. If we wait for threats to fully materialize, we will have waited too long. Our security will require transforming the military you will lead—a military that must be ready to strike at a moment's notice in every dark corner of the world. And our security will require all Americans to be forward-looking and resolute, to be ready for preemptive action when necessary to defend our liberty and to defend our lives.

The "humble" foreign policy Mr. Bush had promised to pursue before he took office ended up buried beneath the ashes of the Twin Towers.

The president's words at West Point announced the coming of a preemption doctrine that would be employed to justify the invasion of Iraq the following year. While the foreign policy establishment was unnerved by Mr. Bush's newly aggressive military stance, most Americans were not. The president's approval ratings remained historically high throughout 2002.

Republicans also enjoyed historic success in the 2002 midterm elections, with the GOP recapturing the Senate despite having a fellow Republican in the White House.

While other Republican presidents had not espoused the kind of unilateral doctrine Mr. Bush outlined at West Point, Democratic presidents had justified American preemption when they felt it necessary to defend U.S. interests.

President Kennedy expressed his version of a preemption doctrine in his Cuban Missile Crisis address on October 22, 1962:

We no longer live in a world where only the actual firing of weapons represents a sufficient challenge to a nation's security to constitute maximum peril. Nuclear weapons are so destructive and ballistic missiles are so swift that any substantially increased possibility of their use or any sudden change in their deployment may well be regarded as a definite threat to peace.

Throughout 2002 and early 2003, the United States prepared for war with Iraq even as we went to the United Nations twice to give Saddam Hussein "a final opportunity to comply with its disarmament obligations."

He refused.

The United States then warned Saddam to leave Iraq before military action commenced.

Once again, he refused.

It was a decision that would cost him his country and his life.

A MISSION WITH ONE HUNDRED FATHERS

On March 19, 2003, the invasion of Iraq was launched. Interestingly enough, the war began with greater bipartisan support than the 1991 Gulf War. George W. Bush entered that war with the approval of such Democratic stalwarts as Bill Clinton, Hillary Clinton, Joe Biden, John Kerry, and John Edwards.

In fact, many of the same Democrats who spent the last six years of the Bush era beating up the president over Iraq were the very ones beating the drum for regime change when Bill Clinton was in the White House.

A cursory review of quotes over the past decade illustrates just how aligned the most powerful Democrats in Washington were with George W. Bush when it came to the threat Saddam Hussein posed to America. The Democratic quotes also show how short our collective memories are as a nation.

Two years before Mr. Bush was even elected to the White House, his predecessor told Americans that their purpose should be to "seriously diminish the threat posed by Iraq's WMD program." President Clinton saw Iraq as a major threat.

Bill Clinton's secretary of state, Madeleine Albright, called the ability of states like Iraq to use their weapons "the greatest security threat we face."

Clinton's national security adviser agreed.

Sandy Berger stated with certainty that "Saddam will use those weapons of mass destruction again, as he has ten times since 1983."

Other Democratic leaders, such as Nancy Pelosi, John Edwards, and Jay Rockefeller, also encouraged military action against Saddam Hussein if war was necessary to eliminate his weapons programs.

One of Mr. Bush's harshest critics during the war, Chairman

Carl Levin, Senate Armed Services Committee, spent the first year of the Bush administration warning the new president of Iraq's grave threat. In 2001, Levin told Mr. Bush that "Saddam Hussein is a tyrant and a threat to the peace and stability of the region. He is building weapons of mass destruction and the means of delivering them."

In 2002, Hillary Clinton also warned that Saddam was working to rebuild his nuclear program and had "given aid, comfort, and sanctuary to terrorists, including al Qaeda members."

Jay Rockefeller, the Democratic vice chairman of the Senate Intelligence Committee, also said in 2002 that "there is unmistakable evidence that Saddam Hussein is working aggressively to develop nuclear weapons and will likely have nuclear weapons in the next five years."

Mr. Bush's 2000 opponent, Al Gore, was quoted in that same year saying that "Saddam has stored secret supplies of biological and chemical weapons throughout his country" and that finding them would be "impossible for as long as Saddam is in power."

Mr. Bush's 2004 presidential opponent, John Kerry, also vouched for Iraq's WMD programs when he told the Senate, "I believe that a deadly arsenal of weapons of mass destruction are in Saddam Hussein's hands and is a real and grave threat to our security."

Even the president's harshest war critic, Senator Ted Kennedy, told fellow senators that "we have known Saddam Hussein has been seeking and developing weapons of mass destruction for some time."

The *New York Times* joined the Democratic chorus by grimly warning of the threat posed by Iraq in the final years of the Clinton administration. The *Times* expressed grave concerns with the dictator's attempt to develop weapons and warned U.S. leaders that negotiations could be ineffective, since "it is hard to negotiate with a tyrant who has no intention of honoring his commitments and who sees nuclear, chemical, and biological weapons as his country's salvation."

On the eve of President Bush's first inauguration, the *Washington Post* was even more apocalyptic, calling Iraq's weapons program the greatest threat facing the new president.

As the Bush administration began its march toward war, many Democrats who feared the great Iraqi threat began changing their tune. Carl Levin went from warning the president about Saddam's WMD to voting against authorizing Mr. Bush to go to war, even if Iraq refused to give up those weapons.

But the waffling chairman was in the minority. The Senate passed its war resolution 77–23. The Republican House followed suit, supporting action against Saddam 296–133.

Most Republicans, including myself, were steadfast in their support for the war. The White House and its conservative allies hoped for a quick victory, a rapid exit, and a transformed Iraq.

This optimistic view was typified by Pulitzer Prize–winning columnist George Will, who told PBS's Charlie Rose in October 2002 that the war would be won quickly and easily, that instability would be good for a region ruled by despots, and that it was cultural condescension to say that the Arab world was not up for democracy.

Mr. Will predicted the Iraq War would trigger a "democratic domino effect," which he considered to be positive. Like many conservatives, Will would later turn against the war and become skeptical that democracy could ever take root there.

The early stages of the war were executed brilliantly. Baghdad fell on April 9 and Mr. Bush all but declared victory aboard the USS *Abraham Lincoln* on May 1, with a "Mission Accomplished" banner framing the backdrop of his remarks.

Though the president received wildly favorable reviews the day of his "Mission Accomplished" speech, that declaration would haunt the Bush White House in the coming years as events inside Iraq began to unravel.

As John Kennedy said following the Bay of Pigs debacle, "Victory has a hundred fathers, but defeat is an orphan." On the day President Bush strode around the *Lincoln* in his flight suit, Republicans and Democrats alike praised the president and the war he had launched.

The media reviews were equally uplifting and, like President Bush, many in the press suggested that the war was over.

Leading up to the president's "Mission Accomplished" speech, the *Los Angeles Times* ran a front-page story with a headline that read, "Iraq Is All But Won; Now What?"

Three days before Mr. Bush put on his flight suit, National Public Radio's Bob Edwards said, "The war in Iraq is essentially over and domestic issues are regaining attention."

PBS's Gwen Ifill praised the president's performance as one-third superhero, one-third movie star, and one-third political icon:

"The president was picture-perfect. Part Spider-Man, part Tom Cruise, and part Ronald Reagan. The president seized the moment on an aircraft carrier in the Pacific."

Even MSNBC *Hardball* host and outspoken war critic Chris Matthews was generous in his opinion of Mr. Bush, declaring in April 2003 that "we're all neocons now." Following Bush's "Mission Accomplished" speech, Mr. Matthews declared, "We're proud of our president."

But over the next few years, George Bush would find himself increasingly isolated. Iraq would go from being an almost universally celebrated campaign to becoming an orphaned operation. And following the outbreak of sectarian warfare in 2006, President Bush never again gained widespread support from Americans for the war.

The same mission that many predicted would be accomplished

in months dragged on longer than World War II. The weapons of mass destruction that even Ted Kennedy and the *New York Times* believed to have existed were nowhere to be found, and Mr. Bush made his political position even more untenable by following his secretary of defense's advice to win in Iraq through the use of a "light footprint."

Adopting Donald Rumsfeld's approach to warfare over General Powell's may have been the president's most fateful decision in the run-up to the war. It was also probably his most misguided, opting for Secretary Rumsfeld's radical, untested doctrine instead of one championed by the man who was sitting in his cabinet, virtually ignored on war-planning matters. It was, after all, General Powell's conservative approach to warfare that had made the First Gulf War such a remarkable success.

Mr. Rumsfeld's obsession with winning wars on the cheap would result in the Iraq War degrading into a long, hard slog.

Years later, it is still difficult to comprehend why conservatives summarily dismissed the approach to warfare they had championed for years. After all, the purpose of the Powell Doctrine was to avoid the type of quagmire the president faced in Iraq. But that is exactly what we did.

The tragedies of Iraq caused conservatives to question their president, the direction of their movement, and how they had allowed their party to go so miserably off course.

FROM RESTRAINT TO RADICALISM

Before the Republican Revolution of 1994, conservative foreign policy was primarily focused on confronting the Communist menace. With the Soviet Union's collapse on Christmas Day, 1991, most conservatives believed America should return to a more cautious, noninterventionist approach to world affairs.

Since the end of World War II, conservative leaders moved between the "realism" of Henry Kissinger and the "idealism" of Ronald Reagan. But the focus throughout the Cold War was always on gaining an advantage over the Kremlin, through either its containment or its destruction.

An early Republican dissenter from the Cold War school of thought was, ironically, the man once known as "Mr. Republican."

Robert A. Taft was a powerful senator, the son of President William Howard Taft, and a strident noninterventionist. Taft championed limited government at home and even more limited government involvement abroad.

The Ohio senator had little use for internationalist projects like the United Nations, the Marshall Plan, or the Truman Doctrine, which proposed the containment of the Soviet Union.

While such a noninterventionist stance would have been a tight ideological fit with the 74 GOP freshmen who took over Congress in 1994, it put Taft out of step with the young congressmen and senators who were elected to office shortly after returning from World War II.

Richard Nixon was one of those war veterans who won his early campaigns in California by accusing opponents of being soft on Communism, going so far as to call one congressional opponent "The Pink Lady."

Once elected, Congressman Nixon used his position on a little-known subcommittee to launch investigations against suspected Communists, building a national platform for himself. Nixon's outing of Alger Hiss as a Communist spy brought him national fame, as well as the wrath of Eastern elites, who never forgave the anti-Communist for destroying their friend's reputation.

Unlike Richard Nixon, Senator Taft and older isolationists were skeptical of the Soviet threat and critical of the Truman administration's internationalist approach. But the debate within the

Republican Party between isolationists and anti-Communists would be short-lived.

In 1952, Taft lost the GOP nomination to Dwight D. Eisenhower, who ended the Korean War by practicing nuclear brinkmanship against the Communist North. Eisenhower's party would remain stridently anti-Communist throughout the remainder of the 1950s.

That anti-Soviet fervor would eventually lead to Wisconsin senator Joe McCarthy's crusade against Communism in the United States. Although McCarthy would, in fact, prove that Communists had infiltrated sensitive positions within the U.S. government, Hollywood, and the American media, his efforts were eventually dismissed as baseless witch hunts.

Public opinion turned suddenly against McCarthy and the Republican majority that was swept into power with Ike in 1952. They would be pushed back into the minority by voters in 1954.

IKE LIKES REALISM

Ike the internationalist moved Republicans away from Taft's isolationism, but maintained a restrictive approach to foreign interventions.

Like Colin Powell a generation later, the former World War II general believed our troops should only be sent to war zones to protect direct threats to U.S. national security. Any decision to use military force overseas would be based only on national security grounds, not moral concerns or nation-building exercises.

Eisenhower's tough realism succeeded in limiting American involvement in foreign wars throughout most of the 1950s. His was a decade of peace and prosperity, restraint and realism.

The next key figure in the arc of conservative foreign policy was Barry Goldwater. Though he was crushed by Lyndon Johnson in a 1964 electoral landslide, the Arizona senator had a profound effect on conservatism and, especially, on a handsome young actor in California by the name of Ronald Wilson Reagan.

Goldwater's foreign policy endorsed extreme tactics like limited nuclear strikes against Vietnam to prevent the spread of Communism across Asia.

Senator Goldwater also framed foreign policy issues in explicitly moral terms. He castigated the Johnson administration as one

> eager to deal with communism in every coin known—from gold to wheat, from consulates to confidences, and even human freedom itself. . . . [W]e must make clear that until its goals of conquest are absolutely renounced and its relations with all nations tempered, communism and the governments it now controls are enemies of every man on earth who is or wants to be free.

Ironically, neocons would charge Ronald Reagan with the same offense almost two decades later. From the earliest days of Reagan's presidency, the same neoconservatives who would later adopt him blasted President Reagan for caring more about trade with the Soviets than crushing the U.S.S.R.

After losing to JFK in 1960 and a gubernatorial race in 1962, Richard Nixon miraculously revived his moribund political career by being elected president in 1968. But President Nixon proved to have a far different approach toward foreign policy than he had as a congressman, senator, or vice president.

After being elected to the White House, President Nixon named Harvard professor Henry Kissinger as his top foreign policy adviser. Nixon, Kissinger, and later President Gerald Ford pursued a policy toward the Soviets known as "détente"—a French word suggesting the easing of tensions.

The Nixon and Kissinger foreign policy team focused less on human rights and moral struggles across the globe than on practicing a realpolitik approach to foreign affairs. Their primary concern was the adoption of policies that were narrowly focused on what was in the best strategic interest of the United States.

The same Richard Nixon who had used red-baiting to beat Democratic political opponents early in his career was now the Nixon who believed diplomatic relations with Communist China and the Soviet Union were in America's best interest.

After Richard Nixon resigned from office in 1974, Gerald Ford continued his former boss's approach of active engagement.

REAGAN'S REALISM

When Ronald Reagan challenged President Ford in 1976, he made Ford's and Kissinger's records on foreign policy a key line of attack. Reagan accused the Nixon White House of turning the United States into a second-rate power, criticized Ford for not meeting with Soviet dissident Aleksandr Solzhenitsyn, and promised to send Kissinger packing if he was elected.

Ford answered Reagan's attacks with political ads suggesting Ronald Reagan was a warmonger.

"Governor Reagan can't get us into war, but President Reagan can," went a Ford TV ad that foreshadowed Jimmy Carter's critique of Reagan four years later. Though Governor Reagan eventually lost to President Ford, the conservative movement remained disenchanted with America's embarrassment in Vietnam and the Nixon/Ford/Kissinger approach to foreign affairs.

Ronald Reagan was elected in 1980, running again on an anti-Communist, pro-freedom platform. Reagan would soon become the most important figure in the history of modern conservatism.

Rhetorically, his foreign policy approach appeared tough, confrontational, and idealist. He rebuilt our national defense, championed the cause of dissidents, and labeled the Soviet Union an "evil empire."

But while his words were idealistic, Reagan practiced foreign policy as a realist.

Reagan faced bitter attacks from neoconservatives early in his administration by initiating overtures to the Soviet Union. In the Middle East, he quickly removed U.S. forces from Beirut after a suicide bombing killed over 200 American troops.

Instead of appearing on TV the day after those attacks and declaring he was going to find those terrorists "dead or alive," the realist in Reagan realized that he neither started the Lebanon civil war, nor would he be able to end it.

As president, Reagan also limited the use of military force to two small events during his eight years in office. Almost immediately after the Beirut attack, President Reagan ordered the invasion of Grenada with the stated goal of protecting U.S. students there. In 1986, he launched his second and final military operation with the bombing of Libya. That attack was in response to a bombing in Berlin that targeted American military personnel.

Arguing that America was exercising its right to self-defense as defined by Article 51 of the UN charter, Reagan said, "When our citizens are attacked or abused anywhere in the world on the direct orders of hostile regimes, we will respond so long as I'm in this office."

Once again, Reagan's rhetoric offered an expansive view of how to use U.S. power, but his actions suggested a more conservative and restrained approach to foreign wars.

Reagan kept relentless pressure on the Soviet Union by supporting liberation movements in countries like Nicaragua while deploying Pershing and Cruise missiles in Europe. So committed was Reagan to containing Soviet expansion that his one major scandal while in office involved the funneling of aid to anti-Communist rebels in El Salvador.

The resulting Iran-Contra affair involved selling weapons to the Iranians and using the profits to prop up anti-Communist rebels in Central America. The actions were illegal. But Reagan's willingness to deal with Iran, the epicenter of terror since 1979, shows just how hardened of a realist the 40th president was.

During his presidency, Reagan was as hated in Europe and across the globe as George W. Bush. Millions marched in the streets of London, Paris, and Berlin to assail the man who would eventually be responsible for the liberation of a hundred million Europeans. But in his time, Reagan was routinely dismissed as a trigger-happy cowboy, unsophisticated, moralistic, and dangerous.

Reagan's record in office was, in fact, nothing of the sort.

Like most conservatives, neocons have claimed Ronald Reagan as one of their own. But their attempt to seize Reagan's mantle ignores the movement's troubled history with the Gipper.

As early as 1982, neocon legend Norman Podhoretz wrote a *New York Times Magazine* cover story titled "The Neoconservative Anguish Over Reagan's Foreign Policy." In the article, Podhoretz's movement attacked Reagan for loving commerce more than loathing Communism.

Neoconservatives also abused Reagan for signing the first arms control pact to reduce the number of strategic weapons in the Cold War. They were equally despondent over Mr. Reagan's decision to remove those Pershing and Cruise missiles he had previously deployed in Western Europe in return for Mikhail Gorbachev removing Soviet SS-20s from Eastern Europe.

While Ronald Reagan aggressively challenged the Soviets rhetorically, he practiced prudence in foreign affairs and actively engaged the Soviets in arms control meetings up until the point Gorbachev demanded the surrender of the Strategic Defense Initiative (SDI). Reagan's refusal to surrender SDI at the 1985 Reykjavík summit was one of the turning points of the Cold War.

Had Gorbachev kept SDI off the negotiating table, Ronald Reagan would have signed an arms control pact in Iceland that would have forever made him a pariah in neocon circles. Instead, the Soviet leader unwittingly launched a series of events that would lead to the dissolution of the U.S.S.R. and transform Reagan into an icon among all conservatives.

But there is no evidence that the neocons' late-blooming love affair with Reagan was anything more than one-sided. Ronald Reagan surrounded himself with realists.

GEORGE H. W. BUSH'S RESTRAINT

Reagan's successor, George H. W. Bush, did not diverge much from the previous administration when it came to international affairs. A former director of the CIA, Bush was an internationalist by instinct and upbringing. Like Reagan, Bush 41 used the American military only twice in foreign wars. The first time was in December 1989, when the United States invaded Panama and deposed the Panamanian dictator Manuel Noriega.

The second use of force was the 1991 Gulf War, which was triggered by Saddam Hussein's August 1990 invasion of Kuwait. Operation Desert Storm brought together the largest international coalition in history and was one of only two wars to have been sanctioned by the United Nations.

The invasion began on January 16, 1991, and served as a massive display of force. Iraq was routed and a cease-fire was declared on February 28, with most of the Iraqi forces in Kuwait either surrendering or fleeing. U.S. casualties were held below 150, as the Iraqi military sustained a stunning and overwhelming defeat.

President Bush was criticized later for not toppling Saddam Hussein's regime and conquering Baghdad. Showing the type of restraint and prudence that had been the hallmark of conservative foreign policy since the Eisenhower era, George H. W. Bush refused to go beyond the internationally agreed-upon mandate of the war and get bogged down in Iraq.

In 1992, Bush 41's secretary of defense, Dick Cheney, came to his commander in chief's defense:

I would guess if we had gone in there, I would still have forces in Baghdad today. We'd be running the country. We would not have been able to get everybody out and bring everybody home. And the final point that I think needs to be made is this question of casualties. I don't think you could have done all of that without significant additional U.S. casualties, and while everybody was tremendously impressed with the low cost of the conflict, for the 146 Americans who were killed in action and for their families, it wasn't a cheap war. And the question in my mind is, how many additional American casualties is Saddam worth? And the answer is, not that damned many.

So, I think we got it right, both when we decided to expel him from Kuwait, but also when the President made the decision that we'd achieved our objectives and we were not going to go get bogged down in the problems of trying to take over and govern Iraq.

SORTING THROUGH A MIDDLE EASTERN MELTDOWN

Many conservatives may wish that Vice President Dick Cheney had paid closer attention to the warnings by then–secretary of defense Cheney, since several of the answers to the question of what went wrong in Iraq can be found in Mr. Cheney's 1992 statement.

How did Iraq become an unpopular war that cost 4,000 U.S. lives, a trillion dollars, and the control of the U.S. House and Senate by Republicans while fostering the meteoric political rise of a one-term liberal senator from Illinois?

The first reason is simple. The war's main rationale proved to be false.

It did not matter that most leaders in America and across the world believed Saddam had WMD. The fact that those weapons were never found crippled the Bush White House politically.

It also did not matter that the United Nations placed the burden on Saddam to prove that he did not have those weapons, or that he intended to restart his WMD program, or that the director of the CIA jumped up in the Oval Office to tell Mr. Bush that the Agency's case against Saddam was a "slam dunk."

In the end, the mistakes of others did not erase the terrible truth that the "slam dunk" case made by CIA director George Tenet vouched for was wrong—tragically wrong. The man who declared himself to be the decider-in-chief knew what Harry Truman had said years ago. The buck always stops with the president of the United States.

America went to war based on false pretenses. The responsibility for that fact fell ultimately on Mr. Bush. The political cost of that incalculable error had an incalculable impact on the conservative movement and the Republican Party.

A second mistake the Bush administration made was its outright rejection of the Powell Doctrine's use of overwhelming force in Iraq. As mentioned earlier, that conservative approach was tossed aside in favor of Donald Rumsfeld's "light footprint" doctrine, which argued that the future of warfare would involve forces who were light and fast.

During the Iraq War's planning, the Bush team believed Rumsfeld's light-and-fast strategy was working in Afghanistan.

Eight years later, President Barack Obama was forced to send thousands of additional troops to that troubled country to quell a resurgent al Qaeda and Taliban. But because of Afghanistan's perceived success in 2001, Rumsfeld's plan to win wars cheaply became the template for Iraq. It also gave a secretary of defense who was already too confident in his abilities even more of a swagger in his step.

Generals once again found themselves fighting the last war—believing that what had worked in the early stages of Afghanistan could be duplicated in Iraq. Time proved them to be wrong.

Rumsfeld entered the Pentagon in early 2001 as a great advocate of "military transformation."

The man who had been secretary of defense a quarter-century earlier used his second tour as SECDEF to lecture generals and admirals on the need to stop thinking about "mass" in favor of "speed and agility and precision."

Rumsfeld's strategic miscalculation on force levels haunted U.S. troops across all of Iraq.

A LIGHT FOOTPRINT LEADS TO HEAVY LOSSES

Barry McCaffrey, who commanded the 24th Infantry Division (Mechanized) during the 1991 Gulf War and now works with me at NBC News, was part of an elite group of retired generals who harshly criticized Secretary Rumsfeld's attempt to win the Iraq War with a "light footprint."

Colin Powell discreetly made his concerns about Rumsfeld's low troop levels known to President Bush at the start of the war and again in 2004. But in both cases, George Bush decided to ignore the advice of the general who had a decade earlier conducted the most ruthlessly efficient military operation in modern history.

The fact that General Powell's historic military success had been achieved in the very same country that Mr. Bush was planning to invade 12 years later made the president's actions all the more disturbing. President Bush told *Washington Post* reporter Bob Woodward that he had never sought General Powell's advice on military planning prior to the Iraq invasion because he knew the former Joint Chiefs chairman had reservations about the coming war.

Perhaps no decision by the 43rd president better illustrates his flawed management style than the decision to exclude General Powell from war-planning discussions. That would, of course, not be politically practical inside a White House where Donald Rumsfeld ran roughshod over anyone who urged caution on the march toward war with Iraq.

Still, how could any serious leader refuse to seek the advice of the world's preeminent expert on warfare in Iraq simply because that general had concerns about the coming military campaign?

Would that not make the General's dissenting opinion even more valuable?

A third mistake of the Iraq War was to assume that once Saddam Hussein was ousted, Iraq would celebrate its liberation, unify its nation, bind up its wounds, use oil revenue to rebuild its country, and become a force for moderation and democratization in the Middle East.

What Mr. Bush and conservatives did not anticipate was the descent of Iraq into disorder, chaos, and looting; the rise of a Sunni insurgency; and the arrival of al Qaeda.

Tragically, U.S. policy helped accelerate this descent by dismantling the Iraqi army and enacting de-Baathification laws. Moreover, the Bush White House miscalculated the degree to which Iraqi society was decimated after three decades of despotic rule and a few months of Paul Bremer's bungled reign.

Power abhors a vacuum, and that is exactly what Mr. Bremer and the Bush administration gave insurgents and terrorists in Iraq. American forces would pay for those 2003 blunders until the arrival of General David Petraeus in 2007.

Many in the Bush administration believed Iraq could be liberated and left alone to govern itself without a major nation-building effort by U.S. forces. But what was created through a military invasion and an incompetent occupation ended up being one of the largest nation-building projects in human history. And the Bush White House and conservatives in Congress were simply ill prepared for that epic task.

A fourth mistake was the neoconservative belief that free elections would lead to unity and political progress, and that, in turn, would lead to security gains. In fact, history proved the opposite order to be true: security became a necessary precondition to allowing political progress to occur in Iraq.

In an environment of chaos and insecurity, elections can actually lead to the hardening of differences between political factions and tribal allegiances.

A fifth mistake was to believe that democracy would be enthusiastically embraced by the Arab world. Iraq, it was believed, would catalyze a fundamental shift in politics in the Middle East, giving rise to moderate forces and a democratic mind-set.

While that has yet to occur, Iraq's 2009 elections showed the rise of Iraqi nationalism and the rejection of many Iranian-backed candidates. In the most recent elections, both Sunnis and Shiites gave their votes to candidates who could deliver on security improvements rather than those aligned with sectarian strife. But predicting any outcome in Iraqi politics has proven over the past decade to be a fool's errand.

Were the Iraq story to have a happy ending, the nation could set in motion a chain of events that could moderate the Middle East over the next generation. But if that were to happen, those developments would owe as much to al Qaeda's overreaching as they would to U.S. involvement in Iraq.

Hopefully, one day historians will conclude that al Qaeda's nihilism coupled with heroic efforts by the U.S. military brought peace and stability to the people of Iraq—changing the country and the region.

Perhaps.

But it is instructive to remember how the high hopes of the "Arab Spring" of 2005 quickly took a grim turn. That was the year when elections were taking place in Iraq and the Palestinian territory, while Syrian forces were being forced to withdraw from Lebanon. Four years later, American policy leaders face a more difficult job in the Middle East, because those democratic elections that were welcomed by the Bush White House resulted in the strengthening of terror groups in Lebanon and the Palestinian territories.

SURGING TOWARD SUCCESS

Despite the multitude of tragic mistakes and inexplicable missteps, the Iraq War may ultimately become a net positive for U.S. national interests.

How could such a thing be possible? In two words: the surge.

President Bush's counterinsurgency strategy was adopted in January 2007, handing off the execution of the plan to the new commanding general in Iraq, David Petraeus.

General Petraeus reversed Mr. Rumsfeld's failed "light footprint" strategy and began forcing his troops to sleep, eat, and live with the Iraqi people. The days of "commuting to work" from forward operating bases was over.

American troops would now clear an area of terrorists, pitch their tents, and stay with the Iraqis. Over time, Petraeus's new approach, as well as al Qaeda's brutal campaign against Iraqi citizens, caused support for U.S. efforts to rise among Iraqis, while al Qaeda's collapsed.

When the surge was adopted, Iraq was on the precipice of widespread civil war. But to President Bush's credit, he withstood withering political pressure from Democrats, the press, and 70 percent of the American public.

Instead of surrendering to that pressure and the suggestion of his top general to withdraw from Iraq, Mr. Bush found the one military leader who believed Iraq could be salvaged.

Mr. Bush doubled down on his Iraq bet and won.

The *New York Times*'s remarkable war correspondent Dexter

Filkins told me that when he went back to Iraq in 2008 after being away for a year, the transformation was so dramatic that he hardly recognized the country.

By every possible metric, the surge worked.

Acts of violence in Iraq were reduced by 80 percent from late 2006. Al Qaeda in Iraq has been obliterated, Shia militia are in retreat, Shiite insurgent Muqtada al-Sadr is in hiding, Iran's influence in Iraq appears to be waning, and Iraq is currently on the road to recovery.

The country that Saddam Hussein ruled for three decades through terror and intimidation is now America's ally instead of its foremost enemy, and its government is both freely elected and accountable to its people in ways it never was under Hussein.

As the Pulitzer Prize–winning columnist Charles Krauthammer has written,

> A self-sustaining, democratic and pro-American Iraq is within our reach. It would have two hugely important effects in the region.
>
> First, it would constitute a major defeat for Tehran, the putative winner of the Iraq war, according to the smart set. Iran's client, Moqtada al-Sadr, still hiding in Iran, was visibly marginalized in parliament—after being militarily humiliated in Basra and Baghdad by the new Iraqi security forces. Moreover, the major religious Shiite parties were the ones that negotiated, promoted and assured passage of the strategic alliance with the United States, against the most determined Iranian opposition.
>
> Second is the regional effect of the new political entity on display in Baghdad—a flawed yet functioning democratic polity with unprecedented free speech, free elections and freely competing parliamentary factions. For this to happen

in the most important Arab country besides Egypt can, over time (over generational time, the time scale of the war on terror), alter the evolution of Arab society. It constitutes our best hope for the kind of fundamental political-cultural change in the Arab sphere that alone will bring about the defeat of Islamic extremism. After all, newly sovereign Iraq is today more engaged in the fight against Arab radicalism than any country on earth, save the United States—with which, *mirabile dictu*, it has now thrown in its lot.

Germany's "Iron Chancellor," Otto von Bismarck, once contemptuously said of our great republic, "God has a special providence for fools, drunks, and the United States of America."

If that is true, nowhere has that providential advantage been exploited more than in the Almighty's absolution of America's muddled military strategy in Iraq. That our U.S. Army and Marine Corps have been able to persevere as well as they have on the battlefield despite years of Washington incompetence could prove to be one of our military's more extraordinary accomplishments.

While Iraq has shown improvement over the past year, nothing is guaranteed in that troubled land. George W. Bush's Iraq War has made fools of foreign policy experts and Washington's best and brightest. The war has humbled both Republicans and Democrats, liberals and conservatives, hawks and doves.

Those predicting a quagmire in the march to Baghdad were wrong.

Those who assured the world that Saddam Hussein had weapons of mass destruction were wrong.

Those promising that America would be greeted as liberators were wrong.

Those predicting that Iraq's elections would dissolve into violence were wrong.

Those predicting that Iraq's elections would bring peace were wrong.

Those who claimed that only America's retreat from Iraq would stabilize that country were wrong.

Those who heaped contempt on George W. Bush for believing a surge would bring significant security gains were wrong.

Those who claimed the surge had failed months after the strategy was implemented were wrong.

And I fear that Barack Obama's promise to remove all U.S. combat troops from Iraq by September 2010 will also be proven to be wrong.

The Iraq War may eventually be "won," and George W. Bush's mistakes there may one day be mitigated by that fact. But any advancements we make there have come at a high cost to our troops, our country, and our movement. While most Iraqis cheered the security improvements the surge brought in 2008, most Americans had already grown weary of a foreign entanglement whose main justification turned out to be false.

After more than 4,000 American deaths and nearly a trillion dollars spent, any gains could be undone in the future by a precipitous withdrawal. As the *Washington Post*'s Tom Ricks concludes in *The Gamble*, the cost of the surge's success may ultimately be U.S. troops spending another decade in Iraq.

FROM RADICALISM TO RESTRAINT

George W. Bush and Republicans were judged harshly by American voters for the mistakes they made during the president's first six years in office. As conservatives now struggle for political relevancy, they should also try to grasp the legacy of Mr. Bush's presidency and his transformation from a humble internationalist who opposed nation building to becoming the champion of assertive nationalism and utopian goals.

Republicans must learn from the mistakes of the past eight years, just as Colin Powell learned from America's tragic involvement in Vietnam.

The central lesson to draw from the last eight years is that dogma and rigid ideology are the natural enemies of conservative foreign policy. There are no easy-to-apply rules to international conflict.

The world is too nasty and brutish a place to elect leaders whose worldview is encumbered by inflexible dogma. Those still believing U.S. troops can be used to export democracy globally or conduct social work on a global scale should be called out as the radicals the past decade has proven them to be.

While a rigid, unyielding approach to foreign policy invites tragic results, there are certain conservative principles that can focus our thinking in the second decade of the twenty-first century.

The classically conservative values that should inform American foreign policy are prudence, restraint, and realism. Those values may be promoted best when conservatives adopt the Weinberger-Powell approach to war.

That doctrine directs U.S. leaders, in part, to use military intervention as a solution to international crises only after all other means of resolving the conflict are exhausted. History has proven that nothing more violently disrupts a nation's social order than warfare. The fact that conservatism is viewed currently as a movement predisposed to militarism is ironic, to say the least. That impression must be changed over time.

Conservative leaders should once again become wary of ideologues who seek to use American troops to promote social policy on a global scale. We should also reject the view of those like former British prime minister Tony Blair, who forcefully argued that America should intervene in failing states like Bosnia and Kosovo—even when there was no vital U.S. interest in the region.

In a significant Economic Club of Chicago speech in April 1999, in which he outlined a "doctrine of the international community," Blair said this of the Kosovo war: "This is a just war, based not on any territorial ambitions but on values. We cannot let the evil of ethnic cleansing stand. We must not rest until it is reversed."

In fact, the NATO intervention in Kosovo in March 1999 was justified explicitly on humanitarian grounds, when the immediate threat was not to other nations but to a country's own population.

I understand the impulse of leaders who want to stop evil and protect innocent human life. Genocide scarred the twentieth century like no other. And while there is much evil in this world, there are only a limited number of U.S. troops.

America's sons and daughters are not capable of ensuring peace and justice for the entire planet. Our army is stretched thin and our bank accounts are emptied.

For too long, the United States has chosen to bear a disproportionate share of the world's security responsibilities. But we have no choice but to begin showing restraint, and backing away from some of our long-standing military commitments.

As conservatives liked to say to flustered Clinton officials in the 1990s, the United States can no longer be the world's 9-1-1.

For over fifty years, the conservative movement has considered the United Nations to be a threat to America's security and sovereignty. But now is the time to dramatically alter our approach to that international body and start using it to our country's advantage.

Since it is in the best interest of the United States to refrain from nation-exhausting wars, conservative leaders should direct all those who wish to advance humanitarian missions through military means to make their case to the United Nations. Americans may decide to play a proportional role in assisting those facing genocide or famine, but our role must be limited and in concert with 150 other nation-states.

The United States of America can no longer afford to bear a disproportionate responsibility securing all four corners of the globe.

THE GUIDING PRINCIPLES OF CONSERVATIVE FOREIGN POLICY

Our goal, then, should be to keep Americans safe and protect U.S. interests across the world when they directly impact our strategic national interests. As a general principle, Washington politicians should leave international moral crusades and global social work to the United Nations and Angelina Jolie.

The second guiding principle conservatives must relearn is the force provision of the Powell Doctrine. Again, General Powell believed that America should only go to war as a last resort, but when we engage, the force applied should be decisive. As Donald Rumsfeld's missteps taught us, trying to win wars cheaply is engaging in a false economy when the war ends up costing America *more* in the end.

Our military strategy for engaging the enemy should be as clear as that of the chairman of the Joint Chiefs on the eve of the First Gulf War.

We should cut our enemies off. We should kill them. And then we should come home.

The third principle the Bush experience taught is that conservatives should treat with great skepticism all those claiming that democracy will transform nations and heal all divisions. I say this as a conservative who was moved to tears with the fall of the Berlin Wall and the liberation of Iraq in 2003.

Democracy is the last, best hope for a dying world. It has advanced civilization throughout the centuries and has made the world a more peaceful and prosperous place. Like Thomas Jefferson, American leaders should swear upon "the altar of God eternal hostility against every form of tyranny over the mind of man."

But conservatives must never forget that the tragedy in Iraq taught us that democracy without security is worthless.

Iraq held three elections in 2005, but found itself racing toward civil war in 2006. While the elections did not cause those ancient divisions, neither did democracy prevent them from widening.

Perhaps at no time were classical conservatives more at odds with President Bush's worldview than when he delivered his second inaugural address. In that speech, he championed a foreign policy doctrine that was anything but conservative.

FREEDOM FROM UTOPIANISM

As he looked west across the Washington Mall, the president proclaimed that his country's "vital interests and deepest beliefs are now one."

George W. Bush then laid out his vision for America's international agenda that he breathlessly promised would bring about "the greatest achievements in the history of freedom."

It seemed surreal that the same man who had championed a limited and modest foreign policy in his first presidential campaign would begin his second term in office by proclaiming that the United States' international policy would now be to promote democracy "in every nation and culture, with the ultimate goal of ending tyranny in the world."

Ending tyranny in the world?

The greatest achievements in the history of freedom?

It was all too much for traditional conservatives.

Ronald Reagan's legendary speechwriter Peggy Noonan took aim at Mr. Bush's Wilsonian pretensions. Noonan, sounding more like Burke than Bush, warned Americans against utopian efforts to turn this imperfect world into heaven. The *Wall Street Journal* columnist also diagnosed the president's condition as "mission inebriation" and counseled the White House to "ease up, calm down, breathe deep and get more securely grounded."

To be fair to President Bush, his rhetoric was not much more expansive than what John F. Kennedy had said in his 1961 inaugural address, when he pledged that America would "pay any price, bear any burden, meet any hardship, support any friend, oppose any foe, in order to assure the survival and the success of liberty."

But John Kennedy's challenge was directed toward one country—the Soviet Union. Mr. Bush, on the other hand, was pledging to wage a righteous war against tyranny itself while claiming a moral mandate to end that scourge across the globe.

The events that unfolded in Mr. Bush's second term exposed the president's 2005 inaugural address as little more than a dangerous fantasy.

Soon after his democratic declaration, free elections advanced the cause of Hamas in the Palestinian territories and the Muslim Brotherhood in Egypt. A year later, democratic elections would help Hezbollah seize more power in Lebanon.

If the road to hell is paved with good intentions, Mr. Bush's newly stated policy provided an express lane for Islamic extremists. The president's belief that democracy could serve as the antidote to Islamic radicalism also ignored the fact that many of the 9/11 terrorists as well as the London 2005 subway bombers were radicalized while living in tolerant European democracies.

The Bush era has taught us that pushing for elections in nations that do not have a history of democracy can be of limited value, or even set back progress.

I again share the views of Charles Krauthammer, who said in 2004,

The danger of democratic globalism is its universalism, its open-ended commitment to human freedom, its temptation to plant the flag of democracy everywhere. It must learn to say no. . . . I believe [the spread of democracy] must be tempered in its universalistic aspirations and rhetoric from a democratic globalism to a democratic realism. It must be targeted, focused and limited. We are friends to all, but we come ashore only where it really counts.

Moving forward, conservatives should be determined to "come ashore" only when it really counts, and unleash decisive force when we do. The U.S. military must be set loose to wage their wars, in the words of historian Walter Russell Mead, at "the highest possible level of intensity."

That approach is the best insurance policy a commander in chief can buy against the possibilities of getting ensnarled in a military quagmire like Iraq or Vietnam.

KNOWING OUR LIMITS

A fourth lesson for conservatives is to understand America's limits.

I believe in American exceptionalism. I also believe a conservative foreign policy approach should proudly acknowledge that America is the greatest force for good in the world.

But conservatives must also acknowledge that the U.S. military is overstretched. The United States is facing a crippling debt, its economy is in crisis, its people are war-weary, and America's days of being the world's watchman are over.

The international community has rapidly moved from being bipolar, to unipolar, to multipolar. It would serve our leaders well to acknowledge this change and exploit new realities to the best advantage of the United States.

And for those who have reflected on the Iraq War and concluded that we should have been more skeptical, cautious, and conservative in our approach, now is the time to relearn the lessons of Edmund Burke, Russell Kirk, and William Buckley.

"Men not being angels, a terrestrial paradise cannot be contrived by metaphysical enthusiasts," warned Kirk in *The Conservative Mind*, "yet an earthly hell can be arranged readily enough by ideologues of one stamp or another."

The world has suffered through enough of those earthly hells over the past century. American conservatives should make it their mission to never again be party to an ideological war.

2 THE GREAT AMERICAN BAILOUT

IN THE AGE OF IDIOTS

> We had a bursting of a bubble and it seems like half
> the strategy of the government is to try to put the bubble
> back. . . . It's odd how this policy is shaping up. The
> stimulus package took a huge deficit and then added a
> massive amount. I can't quite get my head around that idea.
> And now we're seeing the effect of that is frustrating all of
> the longer-term investments we need to make.
> —*Economist Jeffrey Sachs on* Morning Joe, *March 25, 2009*

I'm not sure whether it was the Vicodin or the Valium that was making my head spin, but signing the mortgage papers my Realtor had shoved into my shaking hands was no easy task.

It seems that while I was laid up in bed with a back injury for the last four months of 2004, my wife had become bored, doing little more than waiting to respond to my bloodcurdling screams. Instead of finding a new man who could walk, she settled on a new home that didn't leak.

Susan had helpfully explained to me that our new residence would have a swimming pool for our daughter and a dock for our boat. Luckily for her, I was too disoriented from pain medication to realize that our daughter was too young to swim and our family had no boat.

But those were minor details.

The bigger problem was that we couldn't afford the house.

"Have another Madras, baby," the Realtor cooed before slipping the drink in my left hand and a pen in my right. I dutifully scrawled a big "X" across the signature page and the deed was done.

I had shot the albatross.

It would be weeks before I could crawl to our car and take a trip across town to look at our new home. As soon as I staggered through the front door, I fumbled for my phone.

I was going to call my banker and back out of the deal. Since he had been a friend for 20 years, I skipped the formalities and dove straight into making the complex legal arguments I would surely repeat in a future courtroom battle over whether I had had the mental capacity to enter said mortgage agreement.

Exhibit one would be the drool marks by my signature.

As was my modus operandi while practicing as a skilled courtroom litigator, I began our tense negotiations with my strongest legal argument.

"Dude."

"Dude!"

"Dude, I can't afford this house. Take it back."

"Dude! That's the great thing! Now we have something called an 'interest-only loan' that allows you to buy more home than you can afford."

"But dude, I can't even afford the down payment."

"Dude, that's the most awesome thing about this sweetest of deals. You don't even have to make a down payment."

I must admit, with some embarrassment, that his complex coun-terarguments caught even this seasoned trial lawyer off guard.

My resistance collapsed.

"Sweet. Dude!"

Except for the fact that my banker is so conservative and buttoned-up that he has never uttered the word "dude" in his life, I think the rest of the story is true. I signed papers for a home that was a stretch financially, and when I tried to back out, my banker sold me on a plan where I could manage to buy more house than I could afford.

If my risk-averse, conservative banker had been the only one who got swept up by this twenty-first-century version of tulip fever, we could dismiss it all as the failure of one financial institu-tion. Unfortunately, millions of Americans on both sides of bank-ers' desks were gripped by the same wishful thinking and shortsightedness that drove my deal.

Thankfully, the men and women who negotiate NBC contracts also draw up those legal documents while impaired by Vicodin and Valium. A more sober and less generous front office at 30 Rock might have meant that I too would have been unable to make my mortgage payments after the real estate market collapsed.

Thank God for *Morning Joe*, Mika Brzezinski, and the 90-hour workweek.

For the moment, forget the fact that, like a modern-day Mr. Magoo, I stumbled my way into and out of a risky financial situa-tion. Instead, consider the fact that I had always been so financially conservative that I considered the stock market too dangerous.

Then consider that I had previously been a member of the Judi-ciary Committee in Congress, an attorney who practiced law through two Florida real estate busts, and a small businessman whose mantra had always been that there were no shortcuts to success.

If an experienced attorney, congressman, and businessman

could be pulled into a dangerous home purchase, imagine how easy it must have been for other Americans with no legal training or business expertise to be destroyed by the irrational impulses that fed into the housing bubble.

The pathologies that fed that bubble and eventually created the bailout culture that has gripped Washington and Wall Street over the past year were outgrowths of an American public that had lived beyond their means for years.

By 2008, we were leveraging our personal finances the way Wall Street has always managed theirs.

And why not?

Credit was easy. The dollar was cheap. Consumerism was rampant. Personal savings rates hit zero.

Politicians pressured Fannie Mae and Freddie Mac to expand the housing market. Lending standards were relaxed. Institutions began giving loans to people who couldn't afford them. Banks followed suit.

The housing market became inflated. Home prices skyrocketed. Americans flipped properties. Teachers became Realtors. Accountants became developers. Citizens became speculators. Mortgages became credit cards. Risk spread across the globe.

Politicians became more popular. Wall Street got richer. Americans got fatter.

And then the music stopped.

HOW WASHINGTON WRECKED THE ECONOMY

After the collapse of Lehman Brothers, Washington, Wall Street, and the world tried to comprehend what caused the financial meltdown. President Bush and Treasury Secretary Paulson initially seemed baffled by the cause and extent of the crisis.

The new administration under the guidance of President Obama and Secretary Geithner seemed even less sure of themselves—if that is, in fact, possible.

But like September 11, time provided perspective. Americans would learn later, in both national traumas, that their leaders had missed warning signs that signaled a coming storm.

Even the most ardent supporter of George W. Bush had to flinch when journalists got their hands on an August 2001 CIA report that was titled "Bin Laden Determined to Strike in U.S."

For the housing crisis, such smoking guns were not hidden in top-secret reports, but instead printed on the front pages of America's newspapers.

A September 30, 1999, *New York Times* article announced the easing of credit at Fannie Mae and Freddie Mac. Cassandras warned of the policies' possible consequences, but to little effect.

The article, "Fannie Mae Eases Credit to Aid Mortgage Lending," reported that the Clinton administration had stepped up pressure on the banks to extend risky loans to poorer Americans. The *Times* described the program as one "encouraging banks to extend home mortgages to individuals whose credit is not good enough to qualify for conventional loans."

The *Times*'s Stephen Holmes reported that the policy pushed on Fannie Mae by politicians would require the agency to carry significantly more risk. The change in loan standards could eventually prompt "a government rescue similar to that of the savings and loan industry of the 1980s."

The *Times* then quoted American Enterprise Institute scholar Peter Wallison, who said, "This is another thrift industry growing up around us. If they fail, the government will have to step up and bail them out the way it stepped up and bailed out the thrift industry."

While Wallison warned of the coming collapse for a decade, other national leaders were just as concerned.

In 2002, the Bush White House pressed the Democratic majority in Congress to rein in the reckless habits of Fannie Mae and
Freddie Mac.

Democrats were indignant.

Current Banking Chairman Barney Frank ignored the subprime
warnings, saying that when it came to Fannie Mae, he preferred to
"roll the dice" in favor of home ownership.

New York senator Charles Schumer blasted the Bush White
House for being ideologically chained to free markets.

And California congresswoman Maxine Waters said simply, "If
it's not broke, don't fix it."

But the housing market was broken and the man who sounded
the clearest warning was the lone voice of libertarianism on Capitol Hill, Congressman Ron Paul.

In a 2003 hearing focused on Fannie Mae and Freddie Mac, the
future GOP presidential candidate warned liberal Banking Committee members that their efforts to protect Fannie and Freddie from the
realities of the free market would soon cripple the economy:

> Ironically, by transferring the risk of a widespread credit de-
> fault, the government increases the likelihood of a painful
> crash in the housing market . . . like all artificially created
> bubbles, the boom in housing prices cannot last forever.
> When house prices fall, homeowners will experience diffi-
> culty as their equity is wiped out.

The libertarian leader then predicted that the economic pain
caused by a subprime collapse would be devastating to Americans
and urged members to heed the warnings of then Federal Reserve
chairman Alan Greenspan. Paul said,

> The more people invested in the market, the greater effects
> across the economy when the bubble bursts . . . Even Fed

Chairman Alan Greenspan has expressed concerns that government subsidies make investors underestimate the risk of investing with Fannie Mae and Freddie Mac.

Ron Paul saw the future and predicted the subprime fallout. When Alan Greenspan and other conservatives echoed those concerns, they were dismissed by Fannie Mae's enablers as right-wing ideologues who hated poor people.

Regardless of their agenda and motives, conservatives were right and the angry Left was wrong.

Rather than engage in class warfare battles and racial politics, most Republicans simply backed down. They instead started using increased home ownership for their own political purposes, taking credit for the growing of the "ownership society."

Every American's dream was to own a house, and now by perverting the most basic rules of capitalism, Washington politicians were making American voters' dreams come true.

Unfortunately, their recklessness set off a chain of events that ravaged the world financial system.

These same politicians would later be put in charge of drafting the trillion-dollar bailouts that were aimed at ending the very crisis their foolishness had begun.

Only in Washington.

FAT FANNIE FLATTENS ECONOMY

In 2000, Fannie and Freddie held $2.1 trillion in mortgages and mortgage-backed securities. By 2005, they held $4 trillion. And by 2008, they held nearly $5 trillion. Together, Freddie and Fannie guaranteed or owned roughly *half* of the country's mortgage market.

During the early part of this decade, Freddie and Fannie were not only growing wealthier, they also continued lowering their

lending standards. They did this partly in response to the accounting scandals that hit the lenders in 2003 and 2004 and led to the
departure of top executives—including Fannie Mae CEO Franklin
Raines, President Clinton's former director of the Office of Management and Budget, who collected $90 million in compensation
from 1998 through 2004.

In response, Alan Greenspan, the Bush administration, and
some members of Congress started to question Freddie and Fannie's practices and even its reason for being. The two mortgage
giants justified their subsidized existence by arguing that only
they could help poor people afford homes.

According to Peter Wallison of AFI and Charles Calomiris of
Columbia Business School, Fannie and Freddie "sold out the taxpayers" by financing almost $1 trillion in highly risky mortgages—
and "the most plausible explanation for the sudden adoption of this
disastrous course is the desire to continue to retain the support of
Congress after their accounting scandals in 2003 and 2004."

A *New York Times* story suggests that Daniel Mudd, who succeeded Raines as the head of Fannie Mae, inherited a company
under siege. Congress pressured Mr. Mudd to steer more loans to
the poor, so he did.

> Disregarding warnings from his managers that lenders were
> making too many loans that would never be repaid, he steered
> Fannie into more treacherous corners of the mortgage market,
> according to executives. For a time, that decision proved prof-
> itable. In the end, it nearly destroyed the company and threat-
> ened to drag down the housing market and the economy.

Since Fannie and Freddie accounted for such a large percentage
of all home mortgages, the decision to lower their lending standards had a huge impact on the market and forced other institutions to follow their lead. Furthermore, starting with the Clinton

administration's changes in the late 1990s to the Community Reinvestment Act—a 1977 law that compelled banks to make loans to poor borrowers who often could not repay them—the government actively encouraged and even *required* banks to relax their lending standards to people from lower socioeconomic backgrounds.

Banking Chairman Barney Frank blamed Republicans' concerns over the corrupting of free-market forces on racist impulses. Chairman Frank also suggested that Republicans didn't care much for the poor.

The *New York Times* editorial board joined in the irresponsible, racially tinged attacks, accusing Republicans who criticized Fannie and Freddie of hating minorities and poor people.

"The two mortgage giants were created to help lower-income people buy homes, especially minorities," the *Times* editorial board wrote in 2008. "In the Republican view of politics, that makes them the enemy."

Despite the *New York Times*'s hyperbole, Freddie and Fannie's congressional sponsors perverted the most basic rules of capitalism and allowed a subprime crisis to start a fire that soon swept across America.

Just as Ron Paul had predicted in 2003, the housing bubble eventually burst.

If shameless political shortsightedness can explain how Washington contributed to the economic meltdown, what explains how the best and brightest financial minds on Wall Street were caught without their clothes on when the tide went out?

In a word, greed.

HOW WALL STREET WRECKED THE ECONOMY

For two decades, Wall Street titans raked in outrageous rewards with little risk, despite engaging in the kind of reckless financial behavior that created a dizzying series of booms and busts since 1987. But the one constant of all these economic meltdowns, and the one thing that we can predict about the next one, is that Washington politicians of both parties always found a way to bail out their friends on Wall Street.

That's not populist pabulum. That's just the stubborn fact.

Corporate welfare may come in the form of a $700 billion bailout to rescue America's biggest banks, or it may be a $200 billion bailout of a company like AIG that gives away hundreds of millions in taxpayer-funded bonuses, or it might be a $400 billion bailout of Fannie Mae and Freddie Mac, or perhaps it could involve the rescue of Goldman Sachs, cleverly renamed "The Mexican Bailout Plan."

That 1995 bailout by Bill Clinton authorized a $20 billion taxpayer-funded loan through an Exchange Stabilization Fund to help prop up the Mexican peso. But it actually was a relief bill for Wall Street.

In the latest banking crisis, billions in bailout tax dollars that were supposed to improve the stability of American companies instead passed through those domestic entities to benefit foreign corporations.

For instance, some of the biggest winners in the AIG bailout were not those Connecticut businessmen who were targeted by angry mobs, but instead they were European bankers who made off with $30 billion in congressional bailout money.

France's Société Générale raked in $11.9 billion of American citizens' tax dollars. We also bailed out Germany's Deutsche Bank to the tune of $11.8 billion. And Britain's Barclays Bank made off with $8.5 billion in U.S. bailout relief.

During the last few decades, corporations have also been able to depend on something other than bailouts for their success: the knowledge that the money supply would always be loosened to

curb economic setbacks. This business reality led to what investment bankers called "The Greenspan Put."

Understanding the Greenspan Put helps explain why so many
Wall Street investors began to feel bulletproof when it came to economic loss.

The term "put" is shorthand for "put option," which allows
someone to sell a financial contract to a buyer at a predetermined
price—regardless of that transaction's actual market value.

These put options can become extremely complex, but here's a
simple example of how it works.

Joe buys a stock from Mika for $100.

Mika allows him to pay an extra premium of $5 for a put. The
put is an insurance policy that allows Joe to watch that stock go
down to $50 but still sell it for $75.

That's money well spent by Joe.

The question such an arrangement would raise among sane
people living off of Wall Street would be why Mika would agree to
be the sucker who paid 75 bucks for a stock worth only 50.

The answer is simple. Mika never expected to pay a dime.

Since she sold Joe the stock at $100, and the put option lasted
only a short period of time, the safe bet in normal times was that
stocks would not take a precipitous fall. Therefore, Mika would
pocket her $5, her profits would increase, and her shareholders
would be happy.

But as with all economic bubbles, Mika's actions were based on
the assumption that the market would always move in only one
direction: up. Like most investors on Wall Street during the Age of
Bush, Mika in our example forgot the old adage that what goes up
will eventually come down.

On a more global scale, former Federal Reserve chairman
Greenspan—dubbed "Maestro" by superjournalist Bob Woodward—was long considered the insurance policy against all economic

downturns. Though it is now fashionable to kick Greenspan around, for the past quarter-century, the Fed chairman's ability to ride to the rescue during every financial crisis of the 1990s and 2000s made him an international finance legend.

It also allowed the economy to grow at an unprecedented clip.

The Greenspan Put was simple: when the economy took a dip, the Fed would create enough cheap money (through rate cuts) to get banks out of trouble.

GREENSPAN SAVES THE DAY . . . AGAIN

After the October 19, 1987, "Black Monday" stock market crash triggered the largest one-day percentage decline in our history, Greenspan prevented further damage by pumping liquidity into the economy.

The Fed continued to do so throughout the 1991 Gulf War, the 1994 Mexican peso crisis, the 1997 Asian bond crisis, the 1998 Russian ruble crisis and debt default, the 1998 collapse of the hedge fund Long-Term Capital Management, the Y2K rollover, the burst of the Internet bubble, and September 11.

In every corner of the globe, in confronting almost every financial crisis imaginable, Alan Greenspan was able to work economic miracles. And this, in turn, had a huge psychological impact on Wall Street traders. Leading up to the housing bubble, the Fed's ability to repeatedly ride to the economy's rescue had the unintended consequence of leading investors to believe that whenever things went badly *in the future,* the Fed would lower interest rates, the economy would revive itself, and everything would be fine.

Because Greenspan had been such a masterful captain, guiding our financial ship through narrow passages and around glaciers, investors began to change their behavior.

Wall Street wizards who were arrogant risk-takers by nature believed they were on a summer cruise aboard an unsinkable ship.

Wall Street began spending money and gambling away billions as if they had a put option on *everything* they did. The link between acts and consequences was broken. Since stupid mistakes were backstopped at no extra charge by a cheap dollar and mistakes were mitigated by Greenspan's masterful use of monetary policy, businesses began taking even greater risks and making even bigger mistakes.

It was the financial equivalent of a college student believing he could engage in continuous drinking binges while being protected against hangovers. But to cite William Butler Yeats, the day's vanity would become the night's remorse.

To return to our example, Mika ended up being a sucker for buying Joe's stock at $75 when it was worth only $50, because she didn't earn the $5 profit when the market collapsed. And being armed with a no-cost insurance policy allowed Joe to buy up stocks even if their prospects for profits were not so good. After all, if the stock fell, Joe could just dump his losses on Mika.

Joe thought he was smart. In fact, he considered himself so brilliant in the ways of Wall Street that he believed he was the first of a breed who had learned to take risk out of investing.

Joe and his Wall Street buddies came to believe they now inhabited a world where billions of dollars could be risked without consequences by hiding them in increasingly complex and stupid schemes.

Once you multiply Joe's asinine attitude a million times over, you start to realize why so many things went so bad at once.

Even the former Fed chief's miracle cures couldn't rescue the economy from a subprime meltdown that brought the American economy, and then the world economy, to its knees. And in an

October 2008 congressional testimony, the *New York Times* reported that the Maestro himself was humbled:

> For years, a Congressional hearing with Alan Greenspan was a marquee event. Lawmakers doted on him as an economic sage. Markets jumped up or down depending on what he said. Politicians in both parties wanted the maestro on their side.
>
> But on Thursday, almost three years after stepping down as chairman of the Federal Reserve, a humbled Mr. Greenspan admitted that he had put too much faith in the self-correcting power of free markets and had failed to anticipate the self-destructive power of wanton mortgage lending.
>
> "Those of us who have looked to the self-interest of lending institutions to protect shareholders' equity, myself included, are in a state of shocked disbelief," he told the House Committee on Oversight and Government Reform.
>
> Now 82, Mr. Greenspan came in for one of the harshest grillings of his life, as Democratic lawmakers asked him time and again whether he had been wrong, why he had been wrong and whether he was sorry.

Showing great restraint, former chairman Greenspan did not return the favor by asking Democrats if they regretted ignoring his warnings to Congress about the dangers of promoting loans to Americans who could not afford them. It's a shame Mr. Greenspan did not call them out for their hypocrisy. Because unchastened, those same Democrats who ran roughshod over the most basic laws of free markets then chose to use the ill effects of their actions to attack capitalism itself.

Unfortunately, neither Mr. Greenspan nor any other financial legends were in the mood to lecture Congress on economic realities, on how their lifetime understanding of that system had been shattered overnight.

Even the most revered figures in finance lost their bearings, as banks brought in billions on what Mr. Bush described at a Houston fundraiser as "fancy financial instruments."

The money party on Wall Street was so intoxicating that even financial legends like Clinton treasury secretary Robert Rubin saw their reputation tarnished by the banking collapse of 2008. MarketWatch even listed Secretary Rubin as one of the most unethical businessmen of 2008 for driving Citigroup's business strategy of leveraging massive levels of risk.

After the banking meltdown that had caught even the best and brightest by surprise, Americans were told that the economy's collapse was the result of complicated financial instruments that neither Wall Street giants nor mere mortals could understand.

But one economist described it more simply.

It all seems so complex. But really, it isn't. Enough cards on this table have been turned over that the story is now clear. The economic history books will describe this episode in simple and understandable terms: Fannie Mae and Freddie Mac exploded, and many bystanders were injured in the blast, some fatally.

As home values declined, borrowers defaulted on their mortgages, with investors holding mortgage-backed securities that incurred huge losses.

Investment banks such as Bear Stearns and Lehman Brothers held assets they couldn't sell, ran out of money to meet their obligations, and faced imminent collapse. And that is when our entire financial system began to lock up.

Wall Street and Washington politicians fueled the subprime crisis that wrecked the economy.

Liberal Democrats encouraged negligence at Fannie and Freddie that encouraged similar bad acts among private lenders and American citizens. That, in turn, created the housing bubble.

Republicans in the White House and at the Securities and Exchange Commission turned a blind eye to Wall Street abuses while allowing banks to leverage at dizzying rates of 40 to 1.

Combined, the worst instincts of Democrats and Republicans contributed to create a bubble in the economy that would burst in 2008, causing economic injury to millions of Americans.

But again, after being the architects of the financial sector's economic doom, these same politicians and bureaucrats were then charged with drawing up a trillion-dollar bailout to undo the damage they caused.

HOW WE WRECKED THE ECONOMY

It would be unfair, however, to lay all the blame on the political class.

As George W. Bush would say at the height of the crisis, "Wall Street got drunk and now it's got a hangover."

So let's spread the blame liberally. We can start with the politicians who pressured Fannie and Freddie to make irresponsible loans, and the mortgage giants for acting recklessly, as well as private mortgage companies who greedily rushed in to make billions on a booming housing market, and the Wall Street investors who took the bank loans and chopped them up to spread risk across the globe.

But before we try to assign too much blame to those greedy Wall Street barons and irresponsible Washington politicians, why don't we all take a long look in the mirror and see if we share some of the blame.

Most Americans are intelligent enough to weigh their own financial options and figure out whether they can afford to purchase something as significant as a new home. Like Wall Street's most powerful firms, too many Americans also got drunk over the past decade on cheap money and a booming housing market.

For a while, real estate prices skyrocketed. Homeowners and others flipped houses for profit. And the markets went mad.

In a rush to get rich, thousands became developers, tens of thousands became Realtors, and millions became speculators in a bubble-fed economy.

THE DAY THE MUSIC DIED

Everybody seemed to be getting rich by buying property, renting property, flipping property, selling property, and developing property. It was a "can't-miss" opportunity until the day that it wasn't. And then all hell broke loose.

Pop historians believe the 1960s ended with the death of music fans at the 1969 Altamont Music Festival, which was billed as "Woodstock West."

Altamont's grim legacy was a gathering that was marred by violence, a killing, and several accidental deaths.

It may be a little harder to pin the exact moment last year when we ushered out the halcyon days of hypercredit.

But we do know that when homes stopped selling in the final years of the Bush era, it started a domino effect that ended with a shattered U.S. economy.

Mortgages became delinquent. Speculators panicked. "For Sale" signs began littering neighborhoods. Banks began to foreclose on loans. Credit began to freeze. Businesses started to board up. Americans lost their jobs. More homes went on the market. More homes didn't sell. More foreclosures were entered. Wall Street began to shutter. Bear Stearns melted down. Lehman Brothers collapsed.

Faster than you could say, "Hey, wouldn't it be a great idea to get Hells Angels to run security at our music festival," the Era of Idiots came crashing to an end from Wall Street to Main Street.

When historians try to select a date for when America's finance sector collapsed, it will probably be September 15, 2008, when two Wall Street investment giants were brought low.

Lehman Brothers declared bankruptcy and Bank of America bought Merrill Lynch in a hastily arranged shotgun marriage driven by the Fed.

The Treasury Department's decision to let Lehman die set off unprecedented fear that the collapse of the entire international financial system could follow.

In response, the Federal Reserve seized control of the American International Group (AIG), one of the world's largest insurance firms. The Bush administration quickly followed with a Treasury Department plan called the Troubled Asset Relief Program (TARP).

TARP was created to purchase up to $700 billion in "toxic" securities. By October, President Bush had signed into law a substantially different bill, but one that still constituted the largest intrusion into the economy since the Great Depression.

In explaining his action, President Bush said:

I'm a strong believer in free enterprise, so my natural instinct is to oppose government intervention. I believe companies that make bad decisions should be allowed to go out of business. Under normal circumstances, I would have followed this course. But these are not normal circumstances. The market is not functioning properly. There has been a widespread loss of confidence, and major sectors of America's financial system are at risk of shutting down.

The Republican president then sketched out a scenario in which banks would fail, stock market values would plummet, the value of homes would collapse, foreclosures would rise dramatically, and credit would freeze up, even for people with a good credit history.

But in the end, the bill was a disaster.

STONING PROPHETS FOR SPORT

House Republicans voted against their president's bill and criticized the panicked process by which it was brought to the floor of Congress.

As with the Iraq War and President Obama's 2009 stimulus package, supporters of the TARP bill tried ramming the legislation through Congress by relying on the fear factor. Both the president and Democratic leaders warned of catastrophic consequences if Congress did not immediately pass the bill.

As House Republicans predicted, the $700 billion, three-page bill was poorly thought out and overly ambiguous. TARP ceded too much discretion to politicians and treasury officials.

Because of the House Republicans' concerns, the first TARP bill went down to defeat.

The media's reaction was predictably fierce.

The *New York Times* editorial page accused the "backward-looking Republicans" of threatening the "survival of the nation's financial system."

Conservative *Times* columnist David Brooks angrily railed against House GOP members, even though they turned out to be the only prescient players in the entire TARP drama.

While Arizona congressman John Shadegg appeared on *Morning Joe* to express concern over Treasury Secretary Henry Paulson's "arrogance" and the bill's ambiguous language, Brooks scolded conservatives for their caution and blasted them as "the authors of the revolt of the nihilists."

Brooks then used his September 30 *New York Times* column to accuse those asking the same questions the rest of the media would ask later of being on "a single-minded mission to destroy the Republican Party."

"They have again confused talk radio with reality," Mr. Brooks wrote.

Within a week, Mr. Brooks himself backed off the endorsement of what he had a week before glowingly referred to as "the collective expertise of the Treasury and Fed."

Seven days later, as markets continued their free fall, Brooks tried on the GOP's healthy skepticism for size and became less giddy over the collective talents of Henry Paulson, Timothy Geithner, and Bush.

Soon after thrashing House Republicans for ignoring those men's warnings, he turned around and dismissed the administration's policy responses to the crisis as being little more than "political theater."

Originally, TARP 1.0 was supposed to buy up toxic mortgage-backed securities. But that inspiration never got off the ground. The bailout money began funding the day's latest *ad hoc* idea. Tens of billions of dollars were shoveled into corporations like AIG and Merrill Lynch with a minimal amount of transparency. The names of other financial institutions, like Citi, were kept from public discussions of TARP despite being the motivation for the Wall Street bailout. Other companies like Godman Sachs were big beneficiaries of bailouts since billions passed directly through bailed-out corporations' accounts and directly onto Goldman Sachs' balance sheet.

As the *Wall Street Journal* columnist Holman Jenkins quipped, TARP, the Troubled Asset Relief Program, had become TAMP—the Troubled Asset Multiplication Program.

The White House, treasury officials, and the Fed never appeared to know exactly what they were doing. The waves of improvised rescues directed by the administration and Congress never seemed to have any consistent or even discernible principle.

Bear Stearns? Brokered sale.

Lehman Brothers? Death sentence.

AIG? Multiple rescues.

TARP for automakers? Why not?

Throughout it all, the Bush and Obama administrations' lack of focus shook U.S. markets to their core.

ANARCHY THROUGH AD HOC ACTIONS

"By acting without rhyme or reason, politicians have destroyed the rules of the game," wrote Russell Roberts of George Mason University. "There is no reason to invest, no reason to take risk, no reason to be prudent, no reason to look for buyers if your firm is failing. Everything is up in the air and as a result, the only prudent policy is to wait and see what the government will do next."

"If you put the federal government in charge of the Sahara Desert," Milton Friedman once said, "in five years there would be a shortage of sand."

As if determined to prove Friedman right, a panel of experts created by Congress to oversee the TARP program found that the Treasury Department significantly overpaid for the stakes it took in financial institutions.

According to the *Wall Street Journal*, "An analysis of 10 TARP transactions . . . suggests Treasury paid $254 billion for preferred stock and warrants that may be worth approximately $176 billion, a shortfall of $78 billion." The story went on to say that

> the Treasury mightn't have driven as hard a bargain as private investors. The report says the government's investments and private transactions aren't directly comparable, but that an analysis found that "unlike Treasury, private investors received securities with a fair market value as of the valuation dates of at least as much as they invested, and in some cases, worth substantially more."

As with Republicans' rush to war in 2003 and Democrats' frantic march to pass the 2009 stimulus bill, the TARP bailout proved once again that when it comes to policy that can shape foreign policy or financial systems, haste makes waste.

Because of the unprecedented nature of the crisis, most economic observers believed that doing nothing was not an option. Even the most conservative members of Congress were intimidated by the constant refrain of the Bush administration and Capitol Hill Democrats that inaction would turn this recession into a depression.

Since it is impossible to prove what would have happened had nothing been done, economists will never know whether President Bush and his Democratic allies were correct. But taxpayers do know already that TARP was designed in a way that allowed the same corporations who were saved by huge amounts of taxpayer money to continue to show the same arrogant traits that should have destroyed their companies.

Soon after raking in billions in bailout payments, Merrill Lynch took the unusual step of accelerating its yearly bonus payments to hand out between $3 and $4 billion to its executives and management. These bonuses were paid out despite Merrill's having racked up a $21.5 billion loss in the fourth quarter of 2008—even after a $10 billion contribution from the TARP pool.

Three days later, Merrill was taken over by Bank of America after that merger was itself lubricated by an astounding $20 billion in TARP money.

Merrill CEO John Thain eventually got fired for spending $1.22 million fixing up his office with an $87,784 area rug, a pair of chairs for $87,784, a credenza worth $68,179, and a garbage can for $1,405.

And AIG took billions from U.S. taxpayers before sending their executives to an exclusive retreat in California, where leaders of the broken company could enjoy expensive spa treatments and a vacation from the financial wreckage they had helped create. They were not alone. The arrogance emanating from AIG corporate headquarters only became more pronounced as their economic fortunes became worse.

The corporation, which by March 2009 had 80 percent of its stock owned by the feds, ignored all warnings from Washington and doled out $165 million in "performance bonuses" to the very leaders who destroyed the company and dragged the U.S. economy along for the ride.

Despite President Obama, Larry Summers, and Ben Bernanke expressing their anger over the taxpayer-funded cash payouts, AIG thumbed their nose at the world. They knew they were simply too big to fail.

As the *New York Times* Pulitzer Prize–winning columnist Maureen Dowd wrote of another high-flying executive,

> Sandy Weill, former chief executive of Citigroup, took a company jet to fly his family for a Christmas holiday to a $12,000-a-night luxury resort in San José del Cabo, Mexico. No matter that the company just got a $50 billion federal bailout and laid off 53,000 worldwide.
>
> The interior of the 18-seat jet, as described by The Post, is posh, with a full bar, fine-wine selection, $13,000 carpets, Baccarat crystal glasses, Cristofle sterling silver flatware and—my personal favorite—pillows made from Hermès scarves.
>
> Aux barricades!

But the time for taking to the streets had long passed. Washington's bailout culture had begun with George W. Bush in early 2008, with Barack Obama eagerly supporting Mr. Bush's bailout plans every step of the way. Some of the bigger bailouts have included:

- a failed February 2008 stimulus bill costing $165 billion

- a failed bailout of Fannie Mae and Freddie Mac costing $400 million

- a failed $170 billion bailout of AIG

- a failed $700 billion bailout of Wall Street

- a reckless $800 billion stimulus plan that restarts the American welfare state

- another $750 billion bailout for banks

- another $30 billion to bail out AIG

- and another $634 billion thrown in for good measure to bail out the health care system

After two short months in office, Barack Obama had put policies and promises in place that amounted to a shocking $12.8 trillion in bailout pledges. According to Bloomberg estimates, that is more money than the U.S. GDP for 2008.

Bloomberg also estimated that if the $12.8 trillion that was paid to corporations to fix the housing crisis had gone to paying off mortgages, the government's $12.8 trillion figure would have been able to purchase every home mortgage in America.

"Aux barricades," indeed!

A PERFECT STORM

The Crash of 2008 was the result of a perfect storm of bad policy choices made by Washington, greed-fueled recklessness on Wall Street, and unbridled consumerism on Main Street. The blame should also be shared by Republicans and Democrats, conservatives and liberals, libertarians and socialists of all parties.

Just as Bill Clinton and Barney Frank pushed Fannie Mae to promote reckless subprime loans, George W. Bush and Christopher Cox did little to control Wall Street's ravenous appetite for reckless leveraging that led to billions in bonuses.

It seems ironic that the same Barney Frank who said he favored "rolling the dice" for subprime loans would be chastising bankers and drafting bailouts a decade later.

But that is no more ironic than watching Henry Paulson, who pushed Congress for 40-to-1 leverage ratios while at Goldman Sachs (and made himself hundreds of millions of dollars in the process), serving as treasury secretary when that bureaucracy became entrusted with $700 billion to bring order to the chaos he helped create on Wall Street.

We can leave it to mindless ideologues and partisan pit bulls to assign blame to one party or the other, but in the end, everyone let everyone down.

Perhaps the markets themselves will begin righting our institution's worst wrongs.

After all, natural market selection has already caused many of Wall Street's bad actors to face extinction. In fact, Wall Street as we once knew it is now dead.

A year ago, there were five major independent investment banks.

Lehman Brothers and Bear Stearns have gone the way of the woolly mammoth.

Merrill Lynch survived only because the federal government forced a marriage to Bank of America.

And Wall Street investment powerhouses Morgan Stanley and Goldman Sachs have been reduced to performing much as ordinary commercial banks do. They can accept your deposits and make loans. But expect little more than that for the foreseeable future.

Since commercial banks are regulated far more strictly than

what used to be known as the pure-play investment bank, watch while those outrageous leverage ratios allowed by the Bush administration and the SEC disappear.

Wall Street banks will no longer be allowed to use massive debt to increase the returns on their risky investments. The days of investment bankers investing 30 or 40 times their capital base are over. That will mean less risk, more stability, and fewer market busts.

The current environment has also brought to an end the years of easy credit and cheap money.

Both private citizens and corporate institutions will face more rigorous standards for future loans.

America's savings rate is going to rise in the coming decade to levels not seen since the 1970s. While some may fret that such savings will slow down consumer spending, that is a trend long overdue.

BRINGING ORDER TO CHAOS

To prevent another financial meltdown like the one that exploded in 2008, we must take prudent steps.

We must first increase transparency in our financial markets.

Many of the "instruments of doom" that caused the U.S. economic collapse were sold over the counter in unregulated exchanges. As with Bernie Madoff's $50 billion Ponzi scheme, Chris Cox's Securities and Exchange Commission (SEC) was blissfully unaware of how dangerously the banks were exposed by dealing outside of the New York Stock Exchange or Nasdaq.

The SEC's ignorance was indefensible. But the impact of their negligence was made worse by the fact that too many Wall Street types hid their balance sheet liabilities by using over-the-counter trades.

Clamping down on securities and derivatives trading will make it more difficult for buyers and sellers to turn massive profits. But after years of booms and busts brought on by reckless profit taking, I consider that a positive development.

American financial markets' integrity has made them a magnet for global investment. While their reputation has been badly damaged over the last year, that confidence will be restored moving forward with competent regulators enforcing reasonable regulations that do not cost American jobs.

Passing regulations that promote conservative principles like transparency, prudence, and predictability will, over time, build trust in U.S. markets. It will also sustain our society's order.

Second, regulators should have the authority, when necessary, to ban what are euphemistically known as "new products." While this will result in more conservative, lower-return financial instruments, it will also stabilize markets and protect investors.

Not only were Wall Street's "instruments of doom" used to hide risks in a blizzard of complexity, the banks also were able to use those instruments to bilk consumers. Even highly sophisticated investors couldn't keep up with their brokers' latest schemes.

"Why would anyone want to buy a bond whose return is proportional to the square of the current interest rate?" John Kay asked presciently in the *Financial Times* in 2004. "Why would someone in search of high income buy a security that offers it, but also offers a risk of large capital loss if one of three stock market indices should fall more than 25 percent below its initial level?"

Kay added, "The only people well-equipped to assess the value of these instruments are the people who are selling them."

While making investing instruments more conservative, we should also encourage a return to sanity that has been missing from Wall Street over the last quarter-century.

The institutions that line Wall Street should never again receive advantages from Washington that would allow them to become "too big to fail."

If the crisis of 2008 demonstrates anything, it is that government will always rally on behalf of the biggest, most powerful players. Rules to prevent banks and other financial houses from building the next megaconglomerate like Citigroup would prevent the need for a massive government bailout in the future.

Many Republicans will complain that such a conservative approach to Wall Street would punish success. To be sure, we don't need more legislation like the Sarbanes-Oxley Act, which was single-handedly responsible for driving business from America to London and Dubai.

But conservatives need to learn the difference between being pro-market and being pro-business. We must also remember the lessons of Burke, Kirk, and Buckley that taught us how it is the conservatives' job to bring social order out of chaos.

That means fighting to keep regulations out of small businesses' way, but recognizing that order can be brought to the street only by regulating recklessness out of the system.

Five bubbles in 20 years is enough. It is time to make Wall Street more conservative in its business model and more secure for its investors.

Washington must also stop playing favorites with monster-sized corporations like Citigroup. In a ruthlessly competitive market, Citigroup would not be too big to fail; it would be too big to *succeed.*

Without Washington's protection, Citi would probably be stripped to the bone by thousands of more nimble competitors. The finance company may have started out as one of those nimble players, but over time it became bloated and obsolete, losing the qualities that allowed it to succeed in the first place.

Citi continues to survive only by using its heft and lobbying power to move government to intervene on its behalf and protect it from free-market competition. Whether it lives or dies is in Barack Obama and Nancy Pelosi's hands.

Beyond defending markets in these days of historic intervention, the president and Congress must also limit moral hazard—a term economists have been using since the nineteenth century to describe an environment where investors do not guard against risks because they believe they will be completely protected from them.

The culture of bailouts that is gripping Washington politicians and Wall Street financiers makes it that much more urgent that the message is sent to both Wall Street and Main Street that the Era of the Great American Bailout is about to come to an end.

The most profound and far-reaching solution, of course, is for Americans to start taking greater responsibility for their decisions, being more careful with money, and working toward the day when we can save money the way our parents did.

With the national savings rate inching up from 0 percent in September 2008 to 4 percent today, we may just be on our way.

LET FREE MARKETS BE FREE

Last year, French president Nicolas Sarkozy pronounced, "Laissez-faire is finished." Despite being French, he may be right.

Yet 2008 would have been a very different year had we lived under a laissez-faire system. It was, after all, the U.S. government that worked aggressively over the past decade to undermine the free-market mechanisms of risk and reward that usually contain market excesses.

Reckless subprime loans for the poor and radical leverage rates for the rich violated the most basic principles of capitalism.

Government not only encouraged that risk, government rewarded it.

It was Congress and the White House that pushed Fannie Mae and Freddie Mac to distort the market by handing out loans to Americans who couldn't afford them. And then, when credit markets seized up, Washington couldn't move quickly enough to prop up business failures like General Motors and Fannie Mae. It was as if the feds were producing a business version of *American Idol,* where the worst singers keep getting invited back and never go home.

We often hear that conservatives are champions of deregulation. But if that were the truth, then the Bush administration would have used its majority in the House and Senate from 2003 through 2006 to rein in the abuses of Fannie Mae and Freddie Mac.

Republicans would have also allowed the financial institutions making bad investments to go out of business and let the free market decide the winners and losers instead of Washington politicians. Instead, both Mr. Bush and Mr. Obama joined forces to create this bailout age in which we live.

Of course, the conservative remedy for a bad business's failure is to allow markets to shut it down and make room for more efficient businesses with better management teams and more innovative ideas to take their place.

Conservatives should have told Fannie Mae to let those who could not afford to buy a home rent an apartment. But such laissez-faire thinking was not in vogue over the past decade.

Now we are all paying the price.

One reason conservatives argue for government minimalism is that a hands-off policy allows markets to reward good decisions and punish bad decisions. The tip of the market spear is that it inflicts pain when stupid risks are taken by a business.

Stupid companies die and capital flows to more productive enterprises. That leads to more jobs, an expanding business community, and a stronger nation. But in the land of bailouts, Republican and Democrats alike do all they can to dull that point and let the dumbest actors survive.

The Bear Stearns rescue in March 2008 only put off an essential day of reckoning for Wall Street. While Bear was punished for its failing, the Fed opened its lending window to the other big investment banks. By doing so, it sent the message that a safety net would be provided for the bank's worst bets.

Morgan Stanley, Lehman, Goldman Sachs, Citigroup, and others all concluded that they could ride out the crisis without changing their business models or reducing their leverage.

The Bailout Era was born.

If conservatives are ever going to offer a reform alternative to the bailout chaos, they should start by being honest about how Republicans shared much responsibility.

The housing bubble was brought on by the Federal Reserve's subsidy for debt. It was a money party that was intoxicating for millions of Americans, since home prices shot into the stratosphere and credit was historically cheap.

Between World War II and the 1980s, America's savings rate was close to 10 percent. Since then, it has hovered around 3 percent. Over the last 3 years, our savings rate has fallen to almost 0 percent.

We went from tapping our stock market portfolios, to tearing through cash we made on the Internet boom, to maxing out our credit cards, to using our homes as our fattest credit line yet. In fact, we tapped $1.2 trillion in housing equity over the past 5 years.

The net effect was massive debt, a weakened dollar, and an economy that eventually collapsed.

America can move beyond its bailout culture and rebuild its shattered economy. But it must begin by returning to first principles.

When I was ten years old, my father suddenly lost his job. He had been an industrial engineer at Lockheed for years, and loved that work more than any other he would ever have.

Our family was one of millions of Americans hurt by the recession of the early 1970s. I remember spending part of one summer riding across the South with my dad as he looked for jobs. When we were back home, he would receive $40 a week, which would pay for one tank of gas and groceries.

For the next 18 months, he would continue looking for a job with little luck.

A couple of Christmas mornings were spare, and I remember my older sister crying when she couldn't go places with her high school friends. But other than an occasional reminder, my brother, my sister, and I never noticed my parents were struggling.

Mom and Dad had grown up in the shadow of the Depression with no money, had learned to distrust credit cards, and would buy a car only if they could write a check on the spot.

Growing up, I remember my dad studying a green spreadsheet every few weeks to try to squeeze a few more dollars out of his paycheck. Such behavior would seem compulsive by today's reckless standards. Even in high school, my brother and I quietly told each other that when we got jobs, we would not be as rigid with our finances as our father was with his.

But we were still too young and stupid to realize then that it was my father's conservative stewardship of our family's money that guided us through tough times.

Like my grandmother, who raised four children in rural Georgia throughout the Great Depression, my father knew the value of working hard and saving money.

Those values that got my mom's family through the Depression and my own through a recession are still the principles we need to reignite our country's economy.

America needs to make a clean break from our reckless ways. The time to save is now.

It is also time to put the Age of Fannie Mae, Freddie Mac, Bernie Madoff, Bear Stearns, and Lehman Brothers behind us.

We must return to an economic age when our government erases its debts, Americans balance their checkbooks, and banks loan money to citizens who can afford to pay the money back.

It is time for America and its leaders to begin acting conservative.

3 FROM MEAN TO GREEN

WHY CONSERVATIVES SHOULD CONSERVE

> What is a conservative after all than one who conserves. We
> want to protect and conserve the land on which we live—our
> countryside, our rivers and mountains, our plains and
> meadows and forests. This is our patrimony. This is what we
> leave to our children. And our great moral responsibility is to
> leave it better than we found it.
>
> —*Ronald Reagan*

To my conservative brethren, I would say: Just relax. This chapter is not about Al Gore.

It's not about spotted owls, snail darters, Greenpeace militants, Bobby Kennedy Jr., or tree huggers. I will take no position on global warming, carbon footprints, or how human activity is altering geographic patterns.

That's because I don't have the definitive answer to those questions, and even if I did, I would keep them to myself until you finished this chapter.

Those debates only distract from my larger point, which is that now is the time for American conservatives to go green.

My reasons for breaking ranks with the Republican Party and modern conservative dogma are as simple as they are Machiavellian.

First, an America that conserves energy will be an America that weakens its enemies. Tyrants who run Iran, Russia, and Venezuela will find their jobs more difficult once Americans become less dependent on foreign oil.

Second, the economy that creates, and is driven by, new alternative fuel sources will be the economy that rules the economic landscape for the next generation. The Roman Empire dominated trade through warfare. The British Empire ruled commerce through the seas. America can own the next century by dominating the new wave of energy technology.

The third reason conservatives should go green is that conservatives are supposed to, well, conserve. By definition, we have for the better part of two centuries been the political movement that leans on tradition, preserves the social order, and resists radical change.

With an overwhelming number of scientists agreeing that global warming is a reality, shouldn't conservatives approach the environment with prudence, while conserving the earth's natural order? Shouldn't we do so cheerfully, knowing that doing so will protect the planet, strengthen U.S. foreign policy, and launch the next economic revolution?

Even though Barack Obama failed to follow his own inaugural advice, conservatives should put aside childish things. Now is the time to move past the dogmatic fights of the past. Now is the time for conservatives to embrace environmentalism. Now is the time to transform that movement into a cause that will benefit the three E's: the environment, the economy, and the energy revolution.

And now is the time for conservatives to go green.

It won't be easy. Some on the right will be averse to associating with a movement cluttered by extremists, whose views have been seen as hostile to free markets and U.S. foreign policy. The environmental group Greenpeace spent much of the 1980s organizing massive protests against the very policies Ronald Reagan used to bring down the Soviet empire.

Even today, much of the environmental movement has been hijacked by radicals who seem less concerned with preserving the environment than with attacking those with whom they disagree. Certain strains of environmentalism have devolved into a fanaticism that has fueled the torching of new neighborhoods, the burning of automobiles, and the destruction of private property.

For environmental radicals, their cause has become a quasi-religion that has bred arrogant certitude and doctrinal rigidity.

Left-wing environmentalists have predicted both the coming of an ice age and the specter of global warming in less than a generation.

But conservatives must look past the actions of some bad actors. Despite the misuse of the environment to promote a radical agenda, now is the time for conservatives to claim the cause of conservation.

We should focus on science and technology and let some on the left obsess on tired dogma. Conservatives should be driven by reason and moderation in the fight to protect the planet.

Why?

Because it is both morally right and politically smart.

WASTIN' AWAY AGAIN IN AMERICA

Let's face the facts. The United States of America consumes a disproportionate amount of the earth's energy. Not only is it irresponsible for a country with less than 5 percent of the world's population to burn through 25 percent of its energy supply, it is also stupid.

Our reckless and radical ways only empower enemies across the world.

Over the past quarter-century, the United States has fallen

behind other countries in energy efficiency. While American oil consumption has risen by 20 percent in the United States, it has held steady in Japan and fallen by 25 percent in France and Germany.

We must get smart on the issue of energy efficiency.

It is equally dumb to allow Japan to corner the market on fuel-efficient cars that get over 30 miles per gallon. When I hear politicians whining that the greening of the U.S. auto industry must be approached slowly lest we destroy Detroit, I want to point them in the direction of the nearest Toyota dealership.

The secret to our economic success does not lie below the sands of Saudi Arabia. It may, in fact, rest under the hood of a Japanese car in your hometown.

Sir Paul McCartney has long quoted T. S. Eliot in observing that a good artist borrows; a great artist steals. It is time for American innovators to become great artists in the field of battery technology for cars.

Think about it. The technology should soon exist to choke off the supply of petrodollars to terrorists and Middle East tyrants. What conservative would not be in support of seeking technologies that would cripple America's foreign enemies?

Maybe we have just been unfocused. Maybe the sight of the Twin Towers burning, soldiers marching off to war, and $4.50 gas prices will collectively awaken our country.

The U.S. government has failed to develop an energy policy over the past generation, despite the OPEC oil embargo, the Iranian hostage crisis, and the horrors of September 11. We have known that our failure to plan ahead would place the U.S. economy and foreign policy in the bull's-eye of radical sheikhs and Islamic extremists. But we have chosen inaction instead of decisiveness.

How could we have been so stupid? When will we learn from our mistakes? When will we take advantage of our innate advantages to seize control of our destiny?

The United States of America has the greatest institutions of higher learning on the planet. Eight of the top ten research universities in the world are in our country. Those predicting the economic eclipse of America by a rising China have a stunningly superficial grasp of economic trends.

No country is better poised to dominate the coming technology-driven century than Americans. And the recent weakening in China's economic outlook shows just how dependent that country's growth is on U.S. consumers. China is rising. But China is not our greatest challenge. We are.

The next American Century is ours for the taking.

So what are we waiting for? Why aren't our Washington leaders working late into the night to draw up tax incentives and research grants that would help universities and tech companies develop the next fleet of cars and trucks that will get 100 miles per gallon?

Why are Barack Obama and Nancy Pelosi more interested in rebuilding a failed welfare state than using stimulus packages and massive spending sprees to invest heavily in smart grids and alternative fuel sources?

If Mr. Obama spent more time listening to the likes of Thomas Friedman and less time focused on repeating the mistakes of LBJ, America would again be on the road to economic greatness.

Instead, Americans are stuck with another White House that is oblivious to the fact that the economic world order is changing. Democratic welfare programs will not sustain the U.S. economy any more than supply-side economics. We need instead a new, green economy that elevates our country out of its mounting economic crisis.

Doesn't President Obama realize that the last two wars in Iraq would never have occurred if Saddam Hussein hadn't been sitting in the middle of a region that held most of the world's oil reserves?

Doesn't Barack Obama understand that U.S. troops would

never have set foot on Iraqi soil had that country been sitting on nothing more than sand?

If he does, then why is the president spending so much time rebuilding welfare states of the past instead of investing more aggressively in America's economic engine for the future?

Who do President Obama and George W. Bush think financed Osama bin Laden's attacks on September 11?

Does the 44th president know that the money America and the world paid Saudi Arabian interests for oil made bin Laden's father the wealthiest construction magnate in the Middle East?

Does he know that bin Laden's oil money coupled with contributions from Saudi "charities" helped create the terrorist group that still wants to destroy America?

I would hope that he does. But if he comprehends those facts, why would he focus on welfare solutions rather than energy independence? And with the Congressional Budget Office and the Democratic chairman of the Senate Budget Committee saying that the president has already put America on the path to bankruptcy, Barack Obama may have forever blown the chance to transform America's economy.

Unfortunately, the candidate of change has become the president of the status quo. Barack Obama may have excavated the welfare state to pay off partisan interests, but the trillions he has already spent will ultimately crowd out the kind of aggressive investment America needs to transform its economy and break our dependence on foreign oil.

PAINTING THE PAST GREEN

Now comes the time for a confession.

Many conservatives like myself have long taken a strange pride in the fact that Americans have been rich enough, powerful enough, and tough enough to take what we want, when we want, and how we want. I regularly joke with my liberal friends about owning a fleet of SUVs, and the prime-time news show I hosted before *Morning Joe* had bumper stickers that read, "My other car is an SUV and it's double-parked in Scarborough Country."

That defiance directed toward Al Gore, political correctness, and environmental extremists doesn't seem so funny anymore. And it's not because I stay awake at night worrying about that lonely polar bear floating on a sheet of ice.

It's because I spend my days worrying about America's future.

Though he hasn't been a traditional conservative for years, Senator John McCain set a good example of how a Republican can have a positive impact on the environment. He spent a Senate career being more aggressive on environmental issues than most Republicans—at least until he became his party's 2008 presidential nominee.

Back when McCain was still McCain, he worked to protect wildlife and clean up toxic waste dumps. He cracked down on polluters and preserved vast expanses of pristine wilderness. He was one of the National Parks' best friends in Congress, and he introduced the first Senate bill ever to make a serious investment in green technology.

But then he became a Republican presidential nominee, and the John McCain we knew took a vacation from his record. He abandoned his longtime support for a federal moratorium on drilling along the nation's coastlines. Soon, one of the greenest Republicans in America began holding rallies where his crowds chanted, "Drill, baby, drill!"

McCain even muttered the words a few times, though it seemed to be as soul-crushing to him as standing next to Sarah Palin during his concession speech.

While I will leave the debates surrounding Governor Palin to others, it is obvious that John McCain allowed his environmental-position papers to be ground to dust by the buzz saw of old-style Republicanism.

When winning the hearts of his party's true believers required a shift on the issue, John McCain forgot he was an environmentalist. That was probably because the Republican nominee knew that being green made his conservative base see red.

That has to change.

It shouldn't be a difficult transition.

Most conservatives I know are invested in their communities. Like any smart property owner, they want their hometown to have fresh air, clean water, safe food, and a healthy environment where they can raise their families.

Much has changed over the last generation. Environmentalism has been mainstreamed, and polluters now seem to fall on society's scale somewhere between child molesters and Michael Vick. Many red-blooded conservative males have also been mainstreamed by peer pressure, girlfriends, and a childhood of *Captain Planet.* Others are just selfish enough to want to leave a great inheritance to their children—a world that is better than the one into which they were born.

If conservatives choose the path of conservation, they will reconnect the Republican Party with a past it has too often overlooked.

Republican Theodore Roosevelt is widely considered our first conservationist president. During his term in office, Roosevelt increased our national forests from 42 million acres to 172 million. He founded the U.S. Forest Service.

TR created 51 national wildlife refuges and viewed the chief executive as the steward of our public lands. Teddy Roosevelt considered conservation to be among the most important issues facing our country. And he was a Republican.

"Conservation is a great moral issue," TR said, "for it involves the patriotic duty of ensuring the safety and continuance of this nation."

Beyond Roosevelt, other Republican presidents have signed bills that provided historic protections to the environment. The federal government's most far-reaching actions to protect the environment took place under Republican administrations, from the creation of the Environmental Protection Agency to the Clean Air Act, the Clean Water Act, and the Endangered Species Act.

Even during the Bush years, which were vilified by environmental groups, America's air, land, and water all got cleaner. In fact, according to Gregg Easterbrook of the liberal-leaning Brookings Institution, Mr. Bush significantly strengthened the Clean Air Act to reduce air pollution caused by diesel fuel, emissions from Midwestern power plants, pollution from construction equipment, railroad locomotives, and emissions of methane.

While the Bush era enjoyed modest successes in the environmental field, few would mistake the 43rd president for Teddy Roosevelt.

Part of the reason for Mr. Bush's attraction to oil was probably geographic. Just as I was considered to be one of the greenest conservatives in Congress because my district was filled with protected waterways, George W. Bush's belief that America could drill its way out of its energy woes was based on the fact that he was an oilman who grew up in the heart of West Texas oil country.

While President Bush may have made passing references to clean energy in a couple state of the union addresses, his administration was never focused on conservation. At a 2001 news conference, a White House spokesman was asked if President Bush was concerned that Americans use far more energy per capita than citizens in every other country in the world. The reply?

"That's a big no," the spokesman said. "The president believes it's an American way of life, and that it should be the goal of policymakers to protect the American way of life. The American way of life is a blessed one."

Years later Mr. Bush would finally admit that America's strength was challenged by its addiction to oil. But his administration did too little to address the seriousness of that looming economic crisis.

Too many Republicans in Congress have also been tone-deaf to environmental causes. Often, that opposition was justified because of Democrats' dogmatic approach to the issue. But just as often, Republicans were more motivated on environmental issues by partisan animosity than by a desire to protect America's long-term self-interest.

That's bad policymaking and that's bad politics.

GOING GREEN FOR GOD

Conservatives must now alter their course.

America is going green. Fifty-nine percent of evangelicals consider global warming a serious problem. Only 37 percent of evangelicals tell pollsters they are not concerned.

Conservative Christians have also launched a movement called "creation care," which claims a biblical calling to protect God's creation. Evangelicals are far from alone.

In the United States today, almost 70 percent of Americans say they are concerned about the environment because the earth is "God's creation." Along with more moderate denominations, a growing number of evangelicals now consider environmentalism to be part of a broad Christian moral agenda.

In a 2006 sermon, Pope Benedict XVI warned that "damage to the environment makes the life of the poor . . . particularly unbearable." The pope also called on Christians to unite to care for the earth and expressed support for the Italian church's "day for the safeguarding of Creation." That event calls on parishes across Italy to have believers meditate on ecological damage.

With the greening of even the most loyal part of their base, conservatives must start laying the foundation for a broad, common-sense environment movement and an economic revolution focused on a new energy economy.

Let Democrats obsess over the snail darter. Republicans can take an approach to the environment that is both muscular and moral, by becoming the champions of a green energy revolution that will exploit American innovation and ingenuity for reasons that are selfishly pro-American.

That is a political winner if I have ever seen one.

Great Britain's Conservative Party leader, David Cameron, is also focusing his party on the environment and climate change. He and his aides view it as a "symbol of modernity." And the slogan for Cameron's party, whose color is blue, is "Vote Blue. Go Green, and Save Money."

British conservatives' "go green" strategy is working. After a decade in the wilderness, Tories are making a strong comeback in the U.K.

Conservatives in America must also realize that they have conceded a critical policy issue to Democrats that is only going to grow more urgent in the coming years. If we continue to adopt a head-in-the-sand posture, the GOP will keep losing its grip on voters in critical demographic groups. It seems like such a waste, since those same voters would gladly align themselves with a party willing to fight for environmental reform while simultaneously being pro-growth and pro-jobs.

While in Congress, I won landslide victories in GOP primaries and general elections by being more conservative on fiscal matters than most in my party and being greener on environmental issues than any conservative in Congress. I doubt I ever lost a vote on the right for my environmental stance. But I certainly picked up moderate voters en masse.

That's why I know conservatives can fight to create the economy of the future and protect our planet without indulging standard EPA bureaucratic impulses. We will not throw working-class families into the unemployment lines to accommodate the sleep cycles of the spotted owl. Nor will we force citizens to be battered by byzantine codes and regulations slapped on them by all levels of government.

Conservatives will balance the rights of private property owners with the need to protect America's environmental heritage. We will also set the course for America's next great economic revolution.

It is that innovative decisiveness coupled with the need for a delicate balance that the party of Teddy Roosevelt must strike. Now is the time for conservatives from California to Connecticut to band together to form a distinctly conservative environmental movement that offers a clean break from the old brand of Republicanism.

This new environmentalism will focus on creating jobs and opportunity, on protecting America from its enemies at home and abroad, and on reigniting America's economic engine as the United States races through the twenty-first century.

By selfishly protecting America's self-interest, we will also be protecting the planet lent to us by God.

There is no time to waste. Conservatives must step into the void created by Barack Obama's fateful decision to rebuild the old welfare state, and instead offer the leadership required to save our country and planet. After all, American energy security has never been weaker than it is today.

Energy touches everything we do. It affects how we live, what we eat, how we move from one place to another, the price of everything we buy. Most of the energy we use is generated domestically as electricity—whether it be coal, nuclear plants, windmills, solar technology, biomass, or the rest. But since America is not endowed with self-sufficient oil resources, most oil must be imported.

America consumes nearly 25 percent of the world's oil, even though we hold less than 3 percent of the world's proven reserves. To quote Yeats, "The center cannot hold." An American economic machine that is prone to such excess will soon spin out of control economically and break apart.

MAKING LIFE LESS MERRY FOR MAHMOUD

The future of U.S. foreign policy is tied to its energy policy. Because the price of oil is set by a global commodity market, our economy is held captive too often by worldwide petro-politics.

It has been obvious for some time that America's increasing dependence on oil has all the makings of disaster. In 1973, during the OPEC oil embargo, America imported less than a quarter of its oil. Today, the United States is the largest oil importer in the world.

We import almost 60 percent of our supply. In 2008, this country spent around $700 billion on imported oil. Over the next decade, that number will explode to $10 trillion.

Americans must realize that the bales of cash we ship overseas to keep oil flowing at home ultimately underwrite extremism, aggression, corruption, terrorism, and general global misbehavior. This massive transfer of wealth to the likes of Hugo Chávez, Mahmoud Ahmadinejad, and Vladimir Putin strengthens those regimes and destabilizes the world community.

Two-thirds of all the world's oil reserves is state owned and concentrated in the Middle East. Over the years, OPEC has used collusion to artificially elevate oil prices to exploit America's oil addiction. In 2006, that group of oil-producing nations raked in more than half a trillion dollars from oil exports. Two years later, the windfall had grown to $600 billion.

Saudi Arabia is the crown prince of OPEC. The Saudis are by far the largest oil producers and exporters in the world, and consequently the richest. The House of Saud disposes of its oil capital in part by bankrolling a form of Islamic radicalism that is violent and anti-Western.

The Saudis' radical brand of Wahhabism flows through the arteries of a little-understood network of mosques, religious schools, Islamic centers, and charities that extends from Pakistan to London. Many of those charities and schools are dedicated to good causes. But others serve as fronts that spread propaganda, radicalize poor youths, and finance international terror cells.

American oil dollars support such activities by first being laundered through Saudi Arabia and other OPEC oligarchies before being recycled back to extremists. Eventually that money works itself into the bank accounts of al Qaeda, Islamic Jihad, the Muslim Brotherhood, Hamas, Hezbollah, and their many surrogates.

September 11 showed the horrific consequences of turning a blind eye to America's *de facto* economic sponsorship of oil despots and the terrorists they support. Al Qaeda, after all, was spawned by Saudi start-up money.

Of the nineteen 9/11 hijackers, fifteen were young Saudi men. Osama bin Laden's goal of killing Americans on a mass scale has been funded almost totally by petrodollars from Saudi Arabia and other oil-producing countries.

America gets 16 percent of its oil from the Persian Gulf. But even if it were 1 percent, the danger would still be clear and present. When a region as volatile as today's Middle East becomes the center of the world's oil supply, the United States has no conservative alternative but to use any means necessary to break itself from oil dependency.

As U.S. leaders prepare for the next decade, they must realize that the return of regular economic activity will once again bring exploding demand for global petroleum. No one should take comfort in lower energy prices brought about by an international crisis.

If the Obama administration can stay out of the way long enough to let free-market forces once again spur economic activity, we can then expect China and India to resume the process of hyper-industrialization. When those countries begin growing again at staggering rates, expect energy prices to explode again as well.

The skyrocketing demand for oil is inevitable. In China alone, the number of automobiles will rise from 26 million to 120 million over the next decade. In a matter of years, as many as a billion additional people will be consuming or trying to consume fuel at the same rate that Americans are now.

Absent a prolonged global recession, the era of cheap oil is over. That will remain bad news for Americans until our leaders focus on making energy independence their top economic priority.

And why shouldn't America's independence from petro-fueled extremists be Washington's top priority? It will make the lives of policymakers easier, as it will the lives of all Americans.

Surging energy prices act like a huge tax increase on the economy. The mid-2008 price spike imposed genuine hardships on middle-income and working-class citizens across the country.

Such stark realities mean that America's bedrock problem is reliance on *any* petroleum source, regardless of whether it's pumped in West Texas or Riyadh. If we're going to insulate ourselves from the political and economic menace that oil poses, we ultimately must break free from oil itself.

INVEST, BABY, INVEST

There's no doubt that America could increase its supply of oil by drilling in the Arctic National Wildlife Refuge (ANWR), on the

Outer Continental Shelf, and in the vast oil shale reserves in the Rocky Mountains.

We could also drill off of America's coasts and see very little environmental damage. Offshore drilling is safer than ever. In fact, there has not been a significant spill from an offshore U.S. well since 1969. America's oil producers have pumped 7 billion barrels of oil offshore in the past 25 years, and only one-thousandth of 1 percent (0.00001) has been spilled.

An energy policy based on the partisan chant of "Drill, baby, drill" could stabilize oil prices for a short while without causing significant damage to our coastlines or national parks. But over the longer haul, that approach is just too shortsighted. Washington's leaders must instead look forward and help entrepreneurs, start-up tech companies, and American corporations compete to create the world's future energy supply.

Historically, prosperity has always followed energy. The more affluent a society, the more energy it has been able to consume. The more energy it could afford to consume, the more energy it *did* consume. We now have the chance to make billions off of other countries' consumption by creating the next wave of energy technology.

While America is likely to be more aggressive in efforts to conserve in the future, that does not mean that its move away from an oil-based economy won't require a substitute capable of providing energy on the same scale and volume that oil currently provides.

The bitter truth that environmentalists of every party must face is that nothing at this time measures up to fossil fuel. Even as we work toward the day when America is independent of foreign oil, Washington politicians need to be candid about the challenges our country faces in getting from where we are to where we need to be.

So let's be realistic about where we are going.

The post-petroleum transition process will be long, difficult, and expensive. Oil is so dominant today because it is (1) easily exploited for energy needs, (2) energy-dense, (3) easy to transport, (4) relatively abundant, and (5) relatively cheap in the United States.

As the *Wall Street Journal* put it,

> Currently, alternative sources—wind, solar, biomass, hydroelectric and geothermal—provide less than 7% of yearly domestic consumption. Throw out hydro and geothermal, and it's only 4%. For the foreseeable future, renewables simply cannot provide the scale and volume of energy needed to meet growing U.S. demand, which is expected to increase by 20% over the next two decades. Even with colossal taxpayer subsidies, renewables probably can't even slow the rate of growth of carbon-based fuel consumption, much less replace it. . . . The U.S. has a great deal invested in fossil fuels not because of a political conspiracy or because anyone worships carbon but because other sources of energy are, right now, inferior.

The economics writer Robert Samuelson is equally blunt: "Dependence on foreign oil is unavoidable." Samuelson cited a study by the U.S. Energy Information Administration that forecasts that in 2025, oil will still represent a third or more of total energy use—with more than half imported.

It is important to realize that since energy independence will become a reality only over time, the path to that critical goal will be long. But Washington politicians can't use that reality to avoid our greatest economic challenge ahead.

As oil prices exploded throughout 2008, Republicans mocked Democratic efforts to invest in alternative energy sources because the return on that investment would take too long.

Democrats acted equally irresponsibly by attacking GOP efforts to invest in nuclear energy and to expand domestic exploration. The Democratic naysayers repeated the Republicans' mantra, claiming that the return on nuclear power and additional drilling would take decades.

Guess what happened.

Nothing.

Today we remain as removed from energy independence as we have always been because our political leaders keep hiding behind ideological doctrines to keep our country dependent on oil prices set by Iran, Saudi Arabia, and Venezuela.

Dogmatic radicalism once again trumped reason.

Great job, guys.

America's leaders should take their direction from an order given at the Battle of Mobile Bay when Admiral Farragut shouted to his shaken crew, "Damn the torpedoes! Full steam ahead!"

It is past time for Washington to stop making excuses and start making history.

The good news for a conservative leader who dares to step out of line to reignite his country's economy through green innovation is the fact that energy is infinitely abundant in the sun, the tides, the wind, and the nucleus.

America is also fortunate that the greatest challenge facing those who want to harness this energy is in the area where our country enjoys its greatest advantage—in the scientific and technological quest to harness this energy abundance in a usable form.

Technology moves at the speed of sound in the twenty-first century, and many believe hopeful advances are at the edge of the technological horizon. When the next great discoveries are revealed, will they be found in the university labs and high-tech companies of London, Tokyo, and Beijing? Or will they spring out of American start-up companies from Seattle, Washington, to Miami, Florida, and a hundred points in between?

The answer to that question depends on whether America's leaders have the vision required to face down this great challenge by using government policy to ignite private enterprise.

NEW ECONOMY OR OLD WELFARE STATE?

There are historical precedents.

Soon after the last bombs were dropped on Pearl Harbor in 1941, Franklin Roosevelt began the transformation of Detroit's automakers into the creators of America's arsenal of democracy. Detroit's transformed factories helped crush the Japanese and Nazis.

Sixteen years later, Dwight Eisenhower responded to the orbit of the Soviet satellite *Sputnik* by launching education programs that created a new generation of engineers that transformed America's postwar economy and put a man on the moon. It also created what became known as the "New Math."

Eisenhower faced the Soviet threat by dramatically increasing Washington's investment in scientific research. Funding for the National Science Foundation exploded, and the *Sputnik*-era programs began what would evolve over time into the Internet.

Eisenhower and FDR faced national crises and invested money in the future of the nation instead of on propping up old welfare programs.

One wishes that Barack Obama's Democratic Party would have spent as much energy planning for our economic future as they did refighting old ideological wars of their past. And one can also hope that Republicans who have, at times, reflexively opposed any government involvement in private enterprise realize that following Ike and FDR's lead in fighting for America's future is as conservative an action as a leader can take.

Because of President Obama's and Speaker Pelosi's failings, the road to energy independence will be more difficult. The trillions already spent on partisan programs will be precious dollars diverted from high-paying jobs that could benefit all Americans in the future. That means America has little choice but to double its efforts to curb oil consumption for the sake of our economy and national security.

Energy efficiency simply means doing more with less. Compared with the pioneering work that could take place in high-tech labs, conservation may sound tedious. But these days it looks like conservation may be the smartest, most proven strategy for America to seize control of its energy future.

The United States has saved hundreds of billions of dollars since the 1973 Arab oil embargo, because the price shock that accompanied that crisis encouraged the introduction of new technologies. The energy dollars that would have been wasted otherwise were saved; the oil embargo gave us an economic incentive to design more efficient lightbulbs, engines, appliances, factories, and ways to organize energy use.

While it sounds like a win-win proposition, not all conservatives have been as interested in making energy conservation a national issue. In 2001, Dick Cheney dismissed conservation as little more than "a personal virtue."

But with apologies to the former vice president, saving energy can no longer be considered merely a personal virtue, but rather it must become a public concern. Since the Carter era, we use far less energy per dollar of economic product than ever before. This is unquestionably for the good. Because of that fact, America can produce the same products and earn the same money with one barrel of oil today as with the two or three barrels it once took. That kind of efficiency adds up quickly in a country of 300 million, and makes America more competitive on the world stage.

There are many things Washington can do immediately to transform America in the field of conservation.

Transportation consumes more than two-thirds of the 21 million barrels of oil used every day in the United States, and 97 percent of our transportation consumes oil. Boosting the fuel efficiency of our cars and trucks dramatically would do more to damage terrorists and petro-dictators than anything else we can do right now.

Because the greatest costs of gas-guzzling cars are hidden, car buyers don't value efficiency as highly as they might otherwise. Based on the cars and SUVs that Americans like me prefer, the cumulative savings of fuel efficiency's improvements over time isn't the most important thing on our minds when we go into car showrooms. Buying compact cars is also impractical for consumers like me who are 6'4" and have four children. For fuel-efficient autos to have a significant impact, those models must be extended to light trucks and SUVs.

Domestic fuel efficiency has actually improved by about 60 percent since the 1970s, but those gains have often translated into bigger, more powerful vehicles with more features.

That 60 percent increase in mileage efficiency came in response to a law Congress passed in 1975 requiring automakers to improve fuel economy. At the time, cars averaged only 13 miles per gallon. For the next dozen years, automakers had to keep reaching higher standards.

By the mid-1980s, the average new car got 22 miles per gallon. And what effect did it have? Gregg Easterbrook again: "U.S. petroleum consumption declined from 18 million barrels per day when the CAFE rules were enacted to 15.2 million barrels per day in 1983. That decline broke the OPEC price cartel, and oil prices fell worldwide."

The National Academy of Sciences concludes that without these corporate average fuel economy (CAFE) standards, fuel consumption today would be about 14 percent higher.

Yet from 1988 until 2007, Washington did nothing to promote

higher fuel efficiency. And it was Republicans who fiercely opposed stricter federal fuel-economy standards. This was lunacy. CAFE standards are currently the most important oil-reduction tool in our energy arsenal.

Although a good Washington rule of thumb is that you can never set your expectations for Congress too low, this was depressing even by capital standards.

Conservative environmentalism needs to be employed in the service of an anti–oil fuel economy. The federal government could be useful in this area, aligning market incentives to promote better choices about fuel use.

A great place to start would be for CAFE standards to be pushed forward every few years, eventually reaching 40 miles per gallon by 2015 and 55 mpg by 2025. If Washington once again partnered with Detroit, as FDR did when America faced another transformative challenge, the U.S. auto industry could be rebuilt while its products caused serious pain to petro-dictators across the globe.

Look at it this way: a 40-mpg standard would save more than *50 billion barrels* over the next half-century. A recent McKinsey study likewise found that an international efficiency push could eliminate up to 20 percent of world energy demand by 2020.

Fuel economy isn't an all-in-one solution to the oil problem, of course. Think of energy efficiency as a kind of layover while waiting for a connecting flight. America is currently stuck in an old oil terminal on our way to a destination that is run by green technology. While we are impatient to transform America's economy, we at least should be taking steps to be more efficient, which will make the wait more comfortable.

How long the layover lasts depends on the choices Washington makes over the next few years.

Fuel economy teaches a valuable lesson: successful reforms are often deceivingly simple, causing natural changes in behavior that no sprawling government "initiative" could ever hope to achieve.

It is indisputable that CAFE standards helped speed more efficient cars onto the market, and at a lower price tag. A new CAFE bump could likewise accelerate the production of even better vehicles, including new hybrids and plug-in electrics. Teaming up with a crippled car industry would not only provide hope to Detroit, it would also allow the rest of America to benefit from the more resourceful technologies created in the partnership.

American technology firms, research universities, and scientific laboratories are still the most powerful force for innovation in the world. If our leaders could wisely focus this R&D brainpower on developing a portfolio of oil-replacement technologies the same way the U.S. government teamed with universities during World War II and the space race, it would revolutionize our economy and foreign policy for the next generation.

Government seed money could launch a new energy revolution. Those advances would attract venture capital. That private capital would create opportunities for Americans to thrive in the next great technological wave. Those breakthroughs would make Americans wealthier, healthier, and more secure, while fueling an economic renaissance not seen since troops began coming home after World War II.

All government bureaucracies breed inefficiency. But a decentralized market-oriented environmentalism, combined with the spirit of entrepreneurship, could jump-start the green energy revolution that America so desperately needs.

If the United States became the world leader in designing and manufacturing clean technology and promoting conservation, it could also rebuild the export base that continues to erode each year. And who knows, an environmental conservatism might even defibrillate the larger economy back to life.

These new technologies can work with other underutilized energy sources that already exist. Nuclear power supplies 80 percent of France's energy. While it is expensive, nuclear energy can power entire cities without strengthening international villains or adding to America's carbon footprint.

A long-term approach to nuclear energy would not only reduce the amount of carbon we are putting into the atmosphere, it would also lead to the production of hydrogen-powered cars, while helping America break its dependence on fossil fuels.

Unfortunately, no new reactor has been ordered in the United States since 1978. While we have the technology to keep the reactors safe, our political leaders do not even have the will of the French.

Mon Dieux!

Nuclear power accounts for 20 percent of America's energy usage. Again, the French depend on nuclear plants for 80 percent of their power. There would be 2 billion less tons of carbon in the atmosphere if our percentage were equal to France's. That's 2 billion reasons why anyone who believes global warming is caused by fossil fuels and carbon should want America to go nuclear.

CONSERVATIVES MUST GO BACK TO THE FUTURE

In the 1950s, the conservative intellectual landscape appeared to be a barren wasteland. Literary critic Lionel Trilling asserted in an influential essay, "In the United States at this time liberalism is not only the dominant but even the sole intellectual tradition. For the plain fact is that nowadays there are no conservative ideas in general circulation."

Trilling helpfully added that conservative ideas were simply "irritable mental gestures."

The former Harvard professor's assessments were quickly undermined by the works of Russell Kirk and William F. Buckley.

Kirk and Buckley believed there was a rich conservative tradition in American life.

The great challenge for postwar conservatives was to *recover* that tradition and update it to reflect new circumstances.

In 1953, Russell Kirk's *The Conservative Mind* challenged Trilling and his ilk. Starting with Edmund Burke, Kirk traced the philosophy's intellectual history across generations of America's leaders in a way that connected the conservative movement with the earth.

"The folk called 'conservative,'" Kirk wrote in a later foreword to his book, "join in resistance to the destruction of old patterns of life, damage to the footings of the civil social order, and reduction of human striving to material and production and consumption."

The historical parallel between Kirk's moment in 1953 and the one now facing conservatives on the environment is striking. As it was in Kirk's time, there is recognition of a natural conservative tradition, but it has been lost and must be recovered.

Kirk was an environmentalist ahead of his time.

He wrote that "the spectacle of vanished forests and eroded lands, wasted petroleum and ruthless mining is evidence of what an age without veneration does to itself and its successors."

Precisely *because* he was a conservative, Kirk believed that it was wise to "respect the natural balance in the world." He planted hundreds of trees throughout his life, he said, "as a symbol of our duty to strive for good we may not live to see."

Kirk frequently quoted Burke's sentiment about "the unbought grace of life": the grace that brings us experiences making life worth living, which have a value beyond what can be quantified in money.

Kirk's writings show just how consistent a conservative's reverence for God's creation is with the traditional conservative principles of prudence, responsibility, and reverence.

Ronald Reagan said, "What is a conservative after all but one who conserves. We want to protect and conserve the land on which we live—our countryside, our rivers and mountains, our plains and meadows and forests. This is our patrimony. This is what we leave to our children. And our great moral responsibility is to leave it to them better than we found it."

That should be the goal of every American, be they conservative or liberal.

Our country has the ability to dominate the world economy over the next generation because of the great technological advantage we alone hold. Becoming proactive on a green economic future can help us protect our environment, weaken our enemies, and launch the next great American Century.

"Conservative environmentalist" may sound like an oxymoron today. But it won't soon.

The job of all conservatives is to keep reminding ourselves, "This isn't about Al Gore. It's about keeping America great."

4 WE ARE ALL SOCIALISTS NOW

JE PRENDAI LA MEME CHOSE QUE PIERRE

I always keep a supply of stimulant handy in case I see a
snake, which I also keep handy.

—*W. C. Fields*

You never want to waste a good crisis.

—*Obama chief of staff Rahm Emanuel*

Is capitalism dead?

When that question was asked on the front page of the *Washington Post* on October 20, 2008, I laughed at the *Post* editors for asking such a thing.

I'm not laughing anymore.

The last few months have given even the heartiest defenders of free markets reason to worry that American capitalism may soon be overtaken by a European-style socialism.

Newsweek's editors believe that moment has already arrived.

John Meacham's editor's note of February 16, 2009, put it bluntly.

"Without a great deal of fanfare, the America of 2009 has become a more socialist country."

Meacham drew his conclusion from the fact that the United States was moving toward a more centralized redistributional health-care system, with higher regulation and increased protectionism.

Then there is, of course, Barack Obama's budget that will contain historic levels of spending and debt—even by European standards.

"The numbers are trending in a decidedly French direction," the *Newsweek* editor concluded, "and history tells us that it is far easier to create benefits than it is to take them away."

Meacham is right, of course. The trends *are* disturbing.

My first year in Congress, Bill Clinton proposed a budget that would cost taxpayers $1.6 trillion. Conservatives were shocked at the level of spending that was larded into the Democratic budget and fought hard to keep Mr. Clinton's spending appetite in check. We succeeded.

But by this time next year, President Obama will be running Washington with a spending plan that will force U.S. taxpayers to underwrite a $3.6 trillion budget.

Still, President Obama has seemed determined from his first days in office to resolve a crisis crisis that was created by too much spending and borrowing by responding to the problem with even more spending and borrowing.

Newsweek described Obama's approach as paradoxical. I would call it bizarre.

Along with a budget approaching $4 trillion, a sham stimulus bill approaching another $1 trillion, a $634 billion "down payment" to nationalize health care, a $400 billion omnibus bill, another $750 billion targeted for future bailouts of banks, and a total of $12.8 trillion in bailout payments and pledges, President Obama is now promising to bring a level of debt to Americans that even make Eurozone leaders nervous.

All the while, the percentage of the U.S. economy that is being devoured to fund Washington's destructive spending habits will soon approach numbers not seen since World War II.

On a micro level, Barack Obama has proven himself incapable of exacting any form of fiscal discipline on members of his own party. After spending a year on the campaign trail railing against special interests corrupting Washington, the Democrats' first budget under the "candidate of change" offered a laundry list of reasons that Mr. Obama could be not be trusted any more than Mr. Bush when it came to reining in reckless spending.

The omnibus bill that was passed as a short-term fix in early 2009 saw Congress jam in 8,570 earmarks at a cost totaling almost $8 billion.

With the president claiming that America's economy was teetering on the brink of collapse, the Democratic House and Senate passed critical spending measures targeted toward woody biomass research, a Buffalo Bill historical center, a museum in Las Vegas, the Polynesian Voyaging Society, and approximately 8,565 other similar projects.

House Majority Leader Steny Hoyer admitted on *Morning Joe* that the president's budget unveiled shortly after the omnibus bill was passed contained an additional $8 billion in pork-barrel projects.

REPUBLICANS OUTRAGED BY THE DEATH OF REAGANISM

As the *New York Times*'s Mark Leibovich chronicled earlier this year, Republicans are predictably up in arms.

South Carolina senator Jim DeMint called the president "the world's best salesman for socialism."

Former presidential candidate Mike Huckabee declared that Lenin and Stalin would be supporters of Mr. Obama's spending agenda.

Lenin and Stalin? Really?

Well, if in fact the Age of Socialism has been hoisted upon America, let's at least be intellectually honest about how we got here.

If the Age of Reagan is dead, it wasn't Barack Obama who killed it.

The United States of America has been moving for some time at a quickening pace toward European-style socialism, where government programs consume almost 50 percent of economic activity.

Socialism's cost to European countries has been great.

As *Newsweek* reported in its February 2009 "We Are All Socialists Now" cover story, "More government intrusion in the economy will almost surely limit growth as it has in Europe, where a big welfare state has caused chronic high unemployment."

That looks like the course this country is currently headed.

Meacham and Evan Thomas pointed out that a decade ago, U.S. government spending was 34.3 percent of GDP, while Eurozone countries averaged 48.2 percent. One year into Barack Obama's administration, U.S. spending will reach 40 percent, compared with 47 percent in Europe.

What was a 14-point gap between American capitalism and European socialism at the end of the Clinton era will be cut in half, to 7 percent, early in the Obama administration.

Given the dizzying spending sprees that President Obama and Speaker Pelosi have indulged in throughout the first few months of 2009, there is no reason to believe that the U.S. race to socialism will slow. This is especially true since European leaders are now showing more fiscal discipline than Barack Obama.

But at the risk of being a burr in the saddle of Reagan Republicans who, like Alan Keyes, are ready to condemn Barack Obama as a Communist who must be stopped, let us catch our breath and take a closer look at who began America's long march toward France.

It was a Republican administration that first moved to nationalize the banking and mortgage industry.

George W. Bush's White House also bailed out the U.S. auto industry.

In 2004, Mr. Bush and a GOP majority also passed the biggest expansion of the welfare state since Lyndon Baines Johnson's Great Society. The GOP also allowed domestic spending to skyrocket at rates unseen in a generation.

Defense spending likewise grew at explosive rates, as the military-industrial complex that President Eisenhower warned about benefited greatly from two wars and a White House that refused to make tough choices on weapon systems or wars.

As we try to explain to Americans why we are so gripped by fear and loathing over the staggering price tag of Mr. Obama's spending programs, it might strengthen conservatives' credibility to be honest about the Republican record.

The Age of Reagan collapsed under the weight of GOP mismanagement. Under Mr. Bush, yearly surpluses turned to deficits, Republicans became big spenders, and Democrats called Republican deficits unpatriotic on the campaign trail (while asking for even more money than the GOP in spending bills).

But while it was a Republican who lowered the flag on Reagan's era, it was Democrat Barack Obama who *Newsweek* claims reversed Bill Clinton's ending of big government.

"THE ERA OF BIG GOVERNMENT IS OVER"

I remember sitting in the House of Representatives as President Clinton delivered his 1996 state of the union address to a chamber filled with angry Republicans and embittered Democrats. That night, both sides were participating in that foolish exercise where Republicans would stand up for certain lines while Democrats remained seated, and vice versa.

Of course, in 1996, there were few lines that got GOP representatives out of their seats for a president we believed would be gone in a year.

As Mr. Clinton went through his laundry list of smallish policy prescriptions, conservative firebrands fidgeted in their chairs. Short of calling for the torching of the federal education bureaucracy that night, there was little that the Man from Hope could have said that would have gotten us out of our seats.

But then he said it.

I will always remember the night when Hank Aaron took Al Downing's pitch over the left-field fence for his 715th home run, the first time I listened to The White Album from start to finish with headphones, and the moment the man who had angered me into running for office declared, "The era of big government is over."

It was jarring. Most young Republicans who were sitting with me on the House floor didn't know whether to cheer or laugh, jump from our chairs or remain seated with arms crossed. So we settled on just sitting there looking confused as we stared at Clinton with our mouths agape.

We would hold that pose until the 42nd president left office in 2001.

When President Clinton turned the keys to the White House over to George W. Bush, Americans were spending only 18 percent of their economy on its government.

That was the lowest percentage in 25 years.

But after eight years of Republicanism, federal spending moved up to 21 percent of GDP. The net effect of the Bush and Obama bailout bills will drive that number up to 28 percent by the end of 2009, and as reported above, Washington spending will swallow 40 percent of the U.S. economy in 2010.

THE LONG AND WINDING ROAD TO BRUSSELS

The U.S. government was running a $155 billion surplus the year I left Congress.

Eight years later, that yearly deficit was over a trillion dollars. Bush Republicans also increased the national debt by $5 trillion over that same period.

With Washington blowing through so much money, it is easy to lose perspective on all the dollar figures thrown at you during policy discussions. But if you want to get a grasp on how irresponsible "conservative" Republicans were over the past decade, just remember this: the party of Bush ran up more debt from 2001 to 2008 than the United States of America accumulated from the time of George Washington's inauguration to the day Ronald Reagan became president.

If Mr. Bush's first seven years inched American spending levels closer to Europe's, he spent his last few months in the Oval Office moving the U.S. economy more rapidly toward the Continent.

The Bush administration began its final year signing a $168 billion stimulus package in February 2008.

Mr. Bush then signed a $400 billion bailout of Fannie Mae and Freddie Mac.

Like the February stimulus bill, the Fannie and Freddie bailouts failed. By the end of 2008, Fannie Mae was reporting a $60 billion loss and asking the federal government for another bailout that totaled tens of billions of dollars.

Mr. Bush and his Republican allies on Capitol Hill next bailed out the largest insurance company in America, AIG. That federal government buy-in cost taxpayers $160 billion. AIG then soaked taxpayers for an additional $30 million–plus while paying out $165 million to executives in "performance bonuses."

Today, the U.S. government owns 80 percent of AIG.

By the fall, financial markets were in free fall, and the same in-stitutions that had placed the U.S. economy in such a perilous po-sition came to the Bush administration asking for more money. President Bush and Treasury Secretary Paulson obliged, giving some of Wall Street's worst actors a golden parachute totaling $700 billion.

With America's largest insurance company on the road to na-tionalization, and America's largest banks moving in that direc-tion, it was an obvious next step for President Bush to use federal tax dollars to bail out Detroit.

The Republican who had run as the conservative alternative to Bill Clinton and Al Gore in 2000 had taken over a government with surpluses and turned it into a debt-ridden republic on the march toward European-style socialism.

What George Bush had begun, Barack Obama would see as his mission to complete.

MEET THE NEW BOSS, SAME AS THE OLD BOSS

When Barack Obama was sworn in as the 44th president of the United States, he enjoyed goodwill inside Washington and across the country not seen since John F. Kennedy became president nearly half a century earlier.

The new leader promised to be a candidate of change, and in his inaugural address asked Americans to put childish things behind. He asked Americans to move forward together as Democrats and Republicans.

But while the president was talking about bipartisan compro-mise, his chief of staff was telling reporters that the new adminis-tration would exploit Americans' economic crisis for its own political advantage.

"Never let a serious crisis go to waste," Emanuel said. "What I mean by that is it's an opportunity to do things you couldn't do before."

Rahm Emanuel, a former Clinton aide and Illinois congressman, was a product of Chicago politics. Known for his explosive temper and vulgar language, Emanuel had once famously mailed a fish to a political enemy—sending the message that his enemy, too, would be politically dead.

Now Emanuel would guide Democrats' efforts to take advantage of millions of Americans' suffering to drive a stake into the heart of the kind of economic theories that had been championed by Ronald Reagan and Milton Friedman.

While Emanuel, Pelosi, and President Obama had been given a head start down that path by the Bush administration, Obama Democrats quickly picked up the pace as soon as Mr. Obama was sworn in.

The same president who promised bipartisanship seemed to tire of that political pose after inviting Republican congressmen and senators to a cocktail party and a Super Bowl event.

Once those meaningless social meetings were behind him, President Obama rolled up his sleeves and followed the lead of his staffer who had mailed a dead fish to an enemy.

Perhaps because he knew conservatives would never go along with spending sprees so radical that even *Newsweek* would call them socialistic, the candidate of change became just another Washington politician willing to win political battles at any cost.

President Obama passed the largest spending bill in U.S. history by employing fear, setting up false choices, and engaging in harsh partisanship.

The stimulus package would carry with it a price tag of a trillion dollars after calculating in debt service charges. And the bill would pass after the president warned Americans that the U.S. economy might never recover if it didn't pass.

The *Times* of London later bemoaned the fact that the one thing that American politicians had gotten right over the past twenty years, welfare reform, was destroyed by Mr. Obama's sham "stimulus" bill. Other editorial writers expressed shock at the bill's cost.

To give you a grasp of just how much Barack Obama's first spending bill cost Americans, consider that even in inflation-adjusted dollars, the stimulus bill had a higher price tag than the most expensive government endeavors in our history, including:

- the Louisiana Purchase

- the Panama Canal

- the New Deal

- building the nuclear bomb

- the Marshall Plan

- paving Ike's interstate highway system

- putting a man on the moon

- fighting every war except World War II

In order to pass such a massive bill that bailed out bad actors and excavated the decaying welfare state, President Obama and his Democratic allies had few options but to employ the politics of fear.

FEAR AND LOATHING IN THE OBAMA WHITE HOUSE

"Those who do not remember the past are condemned to repeat it," George Santayana famously said.

Barack Obama would have done well to keep Santayana's

warning close to his heart before trying to scare Americans into supporting his stimulus bill. After all, it was President Bush who had been accused by Democrats like Senator Barack Obama of using fear to sell American voters on the Iraq War.

But President Obama's dire warnings were no less shrill.

The same Barack Obama who had used his inauguration speech as an opportunity to tell Americans that "we have chosen hope over fear," two weeks later told the same country that unless Nancy Pelosi's $800 billion spending bill was passed into law, the U.S. economy would go into a death spiral from which it might never recover.

"A failure to act, and act now, will turn crisis into a catastrophe," the new president told Americans on February 4, 2009.

The only grim scenario that seemed to be missing from the Obama White House's political version of the gothic soap opera *Dark Shadows* was an aide leaking a top-secret intelligence memo suggesting that failure to pass the stimulus bill would result in Saddam Hussein rising from the dead and finally getting his hands on that yellowcake uranium from Niger.

Throughout the stimulus debate, President Obama emulated his predecessor.

Like Mr. Bush, Barack Obama promised to run the White House as a uniter rather than a divider. But as soon as his Super Bowl party broke up, Mr. Obama began playing to his political bases' fears rather than the hopes of Middle America.

The Associated Press reported on the new president's partisan tactics the night of the vote, telling readers that Barack Obama was showing Republicans "a clenched fist on the stimulus bill."

"He's resorting to a sharper tone that is at odds with his vow to make Washington less partisan," noted the AP.

Richard Nixon had always said that Americans vote their fears, and perhaps the disgraced president was right. Barack Obama pushed through the stimulus package using Nixon-style scare tactics while also engaging in harsh partisanship that reduced his political argument down to a crude political justification.

"I won."

That he had. And even if it was troubling for the president of the United States to call political opponents to the White House only to cut off negotiations with such an arrogant declaration, Mr. Obama had in fact won a sweeping victory just a few months earlier.

Still, the same Republican strategists who feared that a centrist Obama administration would doom their party for years to come took delight in the new president's sharp leftward shift. And for good reason. By April 2009, the Pew Poll called Barack Obama the most partisan president in modern U.S. history. No president, including Bush, Clinton, Carter, or Nixon, had divided Americans in their first year as had President Obama.

So much for change.

THE MORE THINGS CHANGE, THE MORE THEY STAY THE SAME

More frustrating for me as a fiscal conservative was listening to Democrats continuing to set up false choices while suggesting that their big spending plans were a break from past political practices.

"We have tried it their way and it has failed," Mr. Obama would tell audiences in the days leading up to the stimulus vote.

But that political claim was just not true.

The new Democratic majority's massive spending plans were nothing new. In fact, they were just a continuation of the ruinous fiscal policies that the Bush Republicans had practiced for eight years.

As Jon Meacham and Evan Thomas noted, the paradox of the Obama approach was that the new president made the decision to "borrow and spend to fix a crisis that was created by borrowing and spending."

Like George Bush before him, Barack Obama decided he would use stimulus spending to pump up a flattened economy. But isn't insanity doing the same thing over and over again while expecting different results?

When the president told Americans that "we have tried it their way," exactly whom was he talking about? And how were past reckless spending policies any different from what the president was now proposing?

Think about it.

If you liked stimulus policies, George W. Bush was your man. He was a politician, after all, who fought two wars, passed massive tax cuts, ran historic deficits, pumped the economy with record increases in defense spending, allowed domestic spending to rise at its fastest rate in a generation, and increased spending on the welfare state by $7 trillion.

George Bush's followers may have liked to think of their leader as a conservative, but Bush Economics owed much more to John Maynard Keynes than to Friedrich Hayek.

Liberals may complain that Bush's tax cuts allowed the rich to get richer, and perhaps they are correct. But the real difference between the Bush and Obama budgets is that the Democratic president intends to reach the spending levels of socialized Europe at a much faster pace.

Unfortunately for conservatives, Barack Obama and George W. Bush's policies have much in common. In fact, both men were inseparable politically, while Washington was wasting more money more quickly than any Washington leaders before.

- Bush and Obama both supported the $168 billion stimulus package of 2008.

- Bush and Obama both supported the $400 billion bailout of Fannie Mae and Freddie Mac.

- Bush and Obama both supported the $150 billion bailout of insurance giant AIG.

- Bush and Obama both supported the $700 billion bailout of Wall Street.

- Bush and Obama both supported the bailout of Detroit automakers.

- Bush and Obama both supported Fed Chairman Ben Bernanke's call for trillions of additional guarantees to Wall Street firms.

- Bush and Obama both supported the call for further trillion-dollar bailouts for banks by Timothy Geithner.

In all, both presidents stood shoulder to shoulder in support of legislation that has rapidly moved the U.S. economy in the direction of Eurozone socialism.

Newsweek's declaration that "we are all socialists now" seems appropriate. But a review of the policies of Republican Bush and Democrat Obama also brings to mind Hayek's dedication in *The Road to Serfdom* to "socialists of all parties."

IN SEARCH OF A STIMULATING SNAKE

While Bush Republicans were as much to blame as Democrats for the bailout culture that gripped Washington in 2008 and 2009, even I doubt my party leaders would have been as reckless with American tax dollars as were Democrats when they began passing spending bills in 2009.

I called their "stimulus" bill "a steaming pile of garbage," while syndicated columnist Charles Krauthammer called the Obama plan "one of the worst bills in galactic history."

It was not the new politics of hope but rather the old politics of spending—legislation larded with pork, special-interest tax breaks, and a 40-year wish list of Democratic programs. This monstrosity was ugly and sprawling, and perhaps the most unfocused spending legislation in American history.

The same presidential candidate who promised to end the old ways of pork-barrel spending was reduced days before the bill's vote to defending a staggering number of special-interest projects by employing the "everyone does it" defense. Matters got worse when almost 9,000 pork projects got jammed into the first Obama budget that approached $4 trillion.

The top Democrat on the Senate Budget Committee, Senator Kent Conrad, expressed concern about the radical spending plans of the president who is a member of his own party.

And Larry Summers, Mr. Obama's top economic adviser, grimly warned that passing a misguided stimulus package that was not timely, targeted, or temporary would cause even greater long-term harm to the U.S. economy than doing nothing. Summers also testified that a stimulus bill should not cause deficits to explode beyond two years.

Like Chairman Conrad, Summers surely had to be concerned with his president's lurch toward socialism through his stimulus plan and historic first budget.

Even the most casual observer of the news cycle must know that Barack Obama's stimulus package failed on all four tests Larry Summers laid out last fall. If we are to believe Summers, that means the Obama stimulus bill may cause more harm to the U.S. economy than good.

The Congressional Budget Office already agrees that is the case.

Soon after the details of the package were released, the CBO director, Douglas Elmendorf, grimly warned that the package would cause such crippling debt that within three years, government spending would crowd out the kind of private investment that would expedite a recovery under normal market conditions.

The CBO director, who was recently appointed by Democrats, then concluded that America's economy would shrink over the next 10 years to a level that would be lower than if President Obama and Speaker Pelosi had done nothing at all.

Of course, doing nothing in a time of crisis is not an option. But the passing of a trillion-dollar bill that will end up shrinking our economy over the next decade shouldn't be an option either.

If President Obama and Speaker Pelosi did not want to listen to Larry Summers, perhaps they should have followed the advice of former Clinton economic adviser Alice Rivlin.

Ms. Rivlin, who served on the Federal Reserve, called for a more targeted stimulus bill that would have cost roughly $300 billion.

But such calls for reason and restraint were pushed aside by a president who said that America's economy would possibly never recover from its crippled state if his stimulus bill was not passed at once.

MORE FEAR AND LOATHING IN THE OBAMA WHITE HOUSE

The continued rush toward Eurozone socialism continued, because Americans were being told the U.S. economy would be forever destroyed if we did not go the way of France. Barack Obama would also justify the passing of a budget the CBO labeled "unsustainable" because of the epic proportions of our economic collapse. But just how unprecedented was the crisis that allowed the Obama administration to move rapidly away from American capitalism?

When Mr. Obama passed his bill, 92 percent of America's workforce was still working. And 90 percent of Americans were still paying their mortgages on time.

Gas prices were trending down, giving U.S. consumers a $2 trillion break in energy over the next year. And the soup lines that were supposed to be winding their way across America were nowhere to be found.

In fact, the only lines anyone could see in New York City during the economic crisis from which Mr. Obama said we could never recover were for $400 iPhones.

If you are old enough to remember the 1980s, you will recall Ronald Reagan's "Morning in America" ad campaign. The gauzy 30-second spots that accompanied that political theme showed farmers pitching hay, steelworkers welding steel, and Americans enjoying a land of plenty.

Things were going so well for America's economy in 1984 that Ronald Reagan won in a historic landslide.

But looking back at the economic numbers from that year shows that unemployment figures were actually higher throughout much of 1984 than they were when Barack Obama declared the coming collapse of America's economy.

Unemployment was even higher in 1982, with 3 percent more Americans out of work. Not to belabor the point, but more people were also out of work in 1975.

And yet, Washington politicians somehow managed to pull Americans out of that mess without nationalizing large segments of the U.S. economy and whipping up fear to pass the biggest spending bill and budget in history.

But the Democratic leaders who were swept into power seemed no more capable of disciplining themselves than the Republicans who ran Washington over much of the past decade.

Socialists of all parties may fight each other on the campaign trail, but when it comes to spending Americans into debt, the only difference recently between Democrats and Republicans is the speed with which they want to spend your money.

DON'T KNOW MUCH ABOUT HISTORY

A fascinating economic debate broke out in the weeks leading up to the passage of the Obama stimulus bill. Conservatives and liberals spent great energy fighting over Obama's trillion-dollar plan by debating the success of an economic program 75 years old.

Washington watched as commentators like George Will and Paul Krugman went back and forth on whether Franklin Roosevelt's New Deal had actually pulled America out of the Great Depression.

For conservatives, drawing battle lines in front of Roosevelt's beloved New Deal was an attempt to discredit the creeping socialism that they saw overtaking the U.S. economy.

To buttress their arguments, conservatives pointed to historically high unemployment rates that gripped America eight years into Roosevelt's presidency.

That was proof enough to some in the movement to conclude that Keynesian economics did not work and that socialist solutions only impeded market corrections that naturally end recessions and depressions.

To further prove their point, they noted that Congress passed and the president signed into law the Economic Stimulus Act of 2008, which amounted to more than $150 billion in stimulus spending. Within four months, the economy was in free fall.

Perhaps even more relevant was the lesson of Japan in the early 1990s.

Like the United States, Japan saw its housing bubble burst, which led to a banking and credit crisis that pulled down the entire Japanese economy. In response, Japan tried stimulating the economy with a huge influx of government spending. In fact, it tried more than a half-dozen stimulus bills.

The result of that massive spending was a recession that lasted 12 years. The spending bills didn't revive the economy, but they *did* create huge deficits that required future tax increases. Those tax increases only further prolonged Japan's economic pain.

While those studies in stimulus spending were failures, most liberals will brush aside conservative protests and cite the success of Franklin Roosevelt's big-government response to the Great Depression. Liberal economists still state with certainty that FDR's New Deal saved Americans from the worst effects of the Great Depression.

But the facts and economic figures of that era do not lie. FDR's spending programs did little over his first two terms to revive the U.S. economy and put Americans back to work.

For half a century, American schoolchildren have been taught that Franklin Roosevelt's New Deal programs magically liberated the United States from the ill effects of the Great Depression. But the fact is that after seven years of the most massive spending programs in U.S. history, unemployment was still hovering at 20 percent.

The same Roosevelt administration that was throwing money at public-works projects to stimulate the economy was depressing it at the same time by raising taxes on businesses that would normally create jobs.

The impact was crippling to private enterprise.

Instead of dollars being spent efficiently in the marketplace, Washington bureaucrats used the billions in a way that actually prolonged the Depression. Socialism failed in the 1930s, conservatives said, and it will fail again.

According to Harold L. Cole, professor of economics at the University of Pennsylvania, and Lee E. Ohanian, professor of economics and director of the Ettinger Family Program in Macroeconomic Research at UCLA,

> The goal of the New Deal was to get Americans back to work. But the New Deal didn't restore employment. In fact,

there was even less work on average during the New Deal than before FDR took office.

Why wasn't the Depression followed by a vigorous recovery, like every other cycle? It should have been. The economic fundamentals that drive all expansions were very favorable during the New Deal. So what stopped a blockbuster recovery from ever starting? The New Deal.

Some New Deal policies certainly benefited the economy by establishing a basic social safety net through Social Security and unemployment benefits, and by stabilizing the financial system through deposit insurance and the Securities Exchange Commission. But others violated the most basic economic principles by suppressing competition, and setting prices and wages in many sectors well above their normal levels.

All told, these antimarket policies choked off powerful recovery forces that would have plausibly returned the economy back to trend by the mid-1930s.

According to Professors Cole and Ohanian,

The main lesson we have learned from the New Deal is that wholesale government intervention can—and does—deliver the most unintended of consequences. This was true in the 1930s, when artificially high wages and prices kept us depressed for more than a decade, it was true in the 1970s when price controls were used to combat inflation but just produced shortages. It is true today, when poorly designed regulation produced a banking system that took on too much risk.

President Obama and Speaker Pelosi believe hiking taxes on Americans who produce jobs and economic growth will promote social justice and egalitarianism. But the New Deal should at least serve as a warning that throwing trillions of dollars of government money at a problem while raising taxes on job creators only increases Americans' misery.

The man who put together Mr. Roosevelt's Depression-era stimulus plan would agree with my conclusions.

Henry Morgenthau was FDR's best friend and his treasury secretary. He monitored the New Deal more closely than anyone alive then or now.

Eight years into the Roosevelt administration's Keynesian gamble, the despondent secretary knew FDR's New Deal was a bust. He went up to Capitol Hill to deliver bad news to Democrats who were growing impatient.

"We have tried spending money. We are spending more money than we have ever spent before and it does not work," Morgenthau admitted. "I say after eight years of this Administration we have just as much unemployment as when we started, and an enormous debt to boot!"

Liberal revisionists have worked furiously of late to argue that Roosevelt's biggest mistake was in not spending *more* money. But serious historians will tell you that any attempts to reframe FDR as a deficit hawk are laughable.

While it failed as an economic strategy, the New Deal did have great merits.

My mother was born in rural Georgia in 1932, during the deepest part of the Great Depression. For her poor family of six, Franklin Roosevelt embodied hope, and his New Deal was a promise from their president that Washington would not sit idle while Americans like my family suffered.

FDR's policies also served to quell social unrest in urban centers, where 25 percent unemployment caused great strains on cities.

But the New Deal's economic failures should serve as a warning

to any policymaker who is more interested in building the next
American Century than winning the next election. The two main
practical effects of massive stimulus plans and tax hikes are likely
to be the retreat of small businesses and the advancement of federal
bureaucracies.

THE DANGERS AHEAD

Both phenomenons will result in less economic activity in the private sector, fewer Americans getting new jobs, less tax revenue
being paid to Washington, and higher deficits for our country to
carry.

Warren Buffett warned of another danger from President
Obama's spending sprees: "These once unthinkable dosages of financial help will almost certainly bring on unwelcome aftereffects.
Their precise nature is anyone's guess, though one likely consequence is an onslaught of inflation."

The Obama administration's trillion-dollar plans to nationalize
parts of the private sector and stimulate the economy may feed
into a short-term consumerism that will slow down the unemployment rate's rise. But in the long run they will crowd out smart investment capital, put us deeper in debt, and fail to grow our
economy over the next decade.

They will also create more dependence on Washington from
corporations, cities, and states.

The Oracle of Omaha also expressed additional concern that
"major industries have become dependent on federal assistance,
and they will be followed by cities and states bearing mind-
boggling requests. Weaning these entities from the public teat will
be a political challenge. They won't leave willingly."

Perhaps breeding that kind of dependence on the centralized
state is exactly what liberal politicians want to do.

But why would other Americans want the same? Why would so

many Americans trust the same federal government who put us in this economic crisis to deliver us from it?

Let's not forget that it was the Democrats and Republicans who were so ignorant of market forces that they pressured mortgage companies and bankers to lend money to people who they knew couldn't afford those loans. It was also these same politicians also allowed Wall Street to leverage their holdings at a preposterous 40-to-1 ratio.

Far from being a break from past leaders, Barack Obama was part of the problem when he was in the Senate. He did little to prevent the financial collapse that helped get him elected president. But he did work aggressively while in the Senate to build a close relationship with power players inside Fannie Mae and Freddie Mac.

Despite not arriving in Washington until 2005, Senator Obama raked in more cash in a shorter amount of time from those scandal-ridden institutions than any other politician in Washington. In fact, his relationship was so close with Fannie and Freddie that of the 99 other U.S. senators serving with Barack Obama, only Banking Chairman Chris Dodd raised more money from Freddie and Fannie over a *20-year time period* than had the candidate of change in two short years.

It's not surprising, then, that he quietly went along with the rest of Washington in enabling the type of bad behavior that wrecked America's economy.

What business board of directors would willingly turn their company over to such a politician?

And why does anyone in the media or on Main Street believe that the same Barack Obama who has never received a single paycheck from a profit-making company his entire life is capable of running the most complex car companies, financial institutions, and insurance companies?

Does any intelligent American really believe that a man so insulated from the free-market system can save that same system?

And does anyone really believe that the same government that took a $155 billion surplus in 2000 and turned it into a $1 trillion deficit a decade later is capable of fixing our current mess?

Balancing the federal government's books in good times is not that complicated. You only spend what you have. But unfortunately for the rest of us, these same politicians ignored basic math and were unfazed by the consequences of their reckless actions.

These politicians who want to run the U.S. economy should know that as the deficit goes up, so does our overall national debt. And as our national debt increases, so do our interest payments. And together, our debt and interest payments choke off the kind of private investment America needs in order to recover from this crisis.

At the beginning of this decade, the national debt was around $5.5 trillion and going down. Today, it is quickly approaching $12 trillion—and it will explode to above $20 trillion before Barack Obama leaves office.

Entitlement programs will only add to our coming crisis. We may soon make Eurozone socialism look like a more conservative bet than Obama-style capitalism.

Rome is being burnt to the fiscal ground by its own leaders. Now these politicians who have failed to pass even the most basic tests of competence desire more power and authority over Americans' checkbooks.

Following Mr. Emanuel's suggestion, they are using a crisis and the fear it is generating to reorder American society in a way that would never have been permitted in more peaceful times.

Wisconsin representative Paul Ryan has written,

The last several months are a foreshadowing of a new era of government activism, rather than an unfortunate but necessary (and anomalous) emergency action. We will soon shift from a market-based economy to a political one in which the government picks winners and losers and extends its reach and power in unprecedented ways. . . . [W]e may be approaching a tipping point for democratic capitalism.

Mr. Ryan has it right. The question now is whether Americans will be willing to fight for economic freedom or instead go the way of France.

5 SOCIAL CONSERVATISM IN THE TWENTY-FIRST CENTURY

Rudd concedes the revolution he had in mind failed. "We lost, they won."

—Tom Brokaw on former 1960s student radical Mark Rudd

The powers not delegated to the United States by the Constitution, nor prohibited by it to the states, are reserved to the states or to the people.

—Tenth Amendment

The mood was electric at the town hall meeting inside the Gulf Breeze High School gym.

Four weeks earlier, I had been swept into Congress along with 73 other Republican freshmen in the GOP landslide of 1994. Now I was taking a victory lap in my Florida district while the Contract with America was steamrolling over Democratic opposition in the U.S. Congress.

"What are we gonna do about this deficit?" one voter asked.

"We're going to force Congress to live by the same rules the rest of us have to live by!" I shouted, punching the air with my fist as the audience took to their feet.

"What about our schools?" another asked.

"Hey! I've got a radical idea," I mockingly said. "Why don't we take money, power, and authority out of Washington's hands and put it back into our classrooms, where the power belongs!"

As I described my legislation to dismantle the federal Department of Education, shouts of approval filled the Florida gym, and I seem to remember torches being lit as effigies of pointy-headed bureaucrats were raised to the rafters.

Emboldened by the audience's energy, an older constituent stood excitedly and shouted, "What do we do 'bout those gay guys getting married in Vermont?"

The question provoked a roar throughout the room that was deafening.

Think Elvis on *Ed Sullivan,* the Beatles at Shea Stadium, or perhaps more appropriately here, the senate scene in *Planet of the Apes.*

I stared at the old man.

Being a newly minted congressman, I tried to choose my words carefully, as any smart politician would. After all, this was a mob—my mob, to be sure, but a mob all the same. And as James Madison warned in Federalist #55, "Had every Athenian citizen been a Socrates, every Athenian assembly would still have been a mob."

After throwing rhetorical gasoline on an open flame for 45 minutes, I doubted that now was the best time to shift strategies and deliver a dispassionate dissertation on the constitutional niceties of federalism.

So I stared at the old man and said nothing.

Silence washed over the gym and I decided to leave my lectures involving constitutional law for another day. Instead, I answered his question with a question.

"What's it to you?"

The old man stared at me as if I had just sprayed his shotgun pink.

Not content with beating the hornet's nest just once, I continued challenging my constituent.

"Why do you care?"

I then leaned toward the microphone and delivered my hastily prepared punch line.

"I've got a plan. Why don't we make a deal with gay guys in Vermont? We won't tell them how to run their lives up there if they don't tell us how to run our lives in Florida."

The old man kept staring as his face scrunched up.

I stared back.

Somewhere in the distance a dog barked.

By now, my decision to go off script had succeeded in sucking all the oxygen out of the room. The gym took on the characteristics of a morgue.

Sweat formed on my brow.

A few more seconds of silence were followed by—could it be?—scattered applause that evolved into a healthy cheer.

The right of gay Vermont men to be left alone by Washington politicians was a small-government principle respected in northwest Florida, a region Jerry Falwell had once called the most conservative place in America.

The fact that this scene also occurred during the most conservative year in modern U.S. history made the event all the more revealing.

CHRONICLING THE CULTURE WARS

The Gulf Breeze town hall meeting was one more reminder that America was engaged in a "culture war" that had been raging for almost three decades. I learned early in my door-to-door campaign for Congress that the election of 1994 was more about refighting the cultural battles of the 1960s than facing the challenges of the coming century.

Since the 1960s, the media have suggested that the culture war was the creation of social conservatives who sought to transform the U.S. government into a Christian theocracy. While this narrative may provide comfort to urban progressives, it is historically wrong.

Social conservatives became fully engaged in America's cultural battles only after absorbing multiple shock waves that sprang forth from the radicalism of the 1960s.

While the 1960s saw great advancements in civil rights as well as women's rights, there were at the same time obvious excesses by the American Left that radicalized our culture and ignited a conservative counterrevolution.

The conservatives' political response to sixties-style extremism would defeat the most radical goals of the liberal movement.

Many reading this book will be too young to remember the sight of college radicals setting campus buildings ablaze. Nor will some remember how images of armed students taking over university buildings flickered across TV screens throughout the 1960s.

In that radical decade, cities burned throughout the night with regularity. Police officers were slandered as "pigs." American soldiers returning from Vietnam were spat upon. Teachers and college professors became targets of contempt. Parents were savaged as oppressors, and God was declared dead.

For millions of Americans, the human cost of the Left's social revolution was too high. While many liberals celebrated the sexual revolution's liberating effects, conservatives were shaken by the explosion in abortions, sexually transmitted diseases, and broken marriages.

The drug revolution, which was glorified by some on the Left as a path to self-discovery, fueled an enormous increase in crime rates, dysfunctional families, and social anarchy.

And the federal government's "war on poverty" had the unintended impact of creating widespread dependence on government. Lyndon Johnson's Great Society worsened rather than helped the condition of the poor and disadvantaged, as urban blight brought on by left-wing social policy created inner-city crises unmatched in American history.

It is why so many of today's conservatives are concerned with President Obama's efforts to revive LBJ's failed welfare state.

While many in Hollywood, academia, and the mainstream media romanticized the social upheavals of the 1960s, millions of Americans living west of the Hudson River and east of Las Vegas were shaken by the dramatic changes they saw unfolding in their schools, on their streets, and in their daily lives.

That was the cultural backdrop at the time. But three issues in particular galvanized social conservatives into political action in the 1970s:

- busing, which forced young children to go to schools outside their local neighborhoods in an effort to promote integration

- campus radicalism, where some of the most disturbing developments occurred, often at state schools that were funded by taxpayers

- the 1973 *Roe v. Wade* decision

The *Roe* decision invented a constitutional right for women to have abortions and voided existing abortion laws across America. It was an act of "raw judicial power," to quote from the dissent of Justice Byron White, and caused social and Christian conservatives to rethink fundamentally their indifference toward politics.

The net effect of a growing cultural decay and a Supreme Court actively engaged in America's culture wars awakened millions of conservative voters.

The New Left may have launched the culture wars from Washington, New York, and Los Angeles, but conservatives soon began a cultural counterrevolution that gained its power from America's heartland.

The *Roe* decision raised the greatest suspicions of conservatives toward the Supreme Court.

A government "of the people, by the people, for the people" seemed to be transformed into a government "of the judges, by the judges, for the judges." Political issues that had been resolved for two centuries on the local level were now being co-opted and federalized by a progressive Court.

As a result, social and religious conservatives became engaged in what Harvard professor Nathan Glazer described as a "defensive offensive."

Evangelicals of all faiths were no longer willing to tolerate the aggressive imposition of views that threatened their way of life, challenged their faith, and did violence to their belief system.

In the moment that *Roe* was handed down, everything changed. Social conservatives who had previously kept their distance from politics would now become intensely engaged. Suddenly, issues the Left had taken on like abortion, school prayer, and gay rights became the center of the political debate.

Because the Left had become so actively involved in America's cultural agenda, the federal government and national politicians started becoming drawn into areas that had previously been beyond their natural jurisdiction.

For two centuries, Washington had been the center of political power in America. After the 1960s, it unfortunately became the center of cultural conflict as well.

By 1980, millions of conservative Americans were ready to launch a more focused counteroffensive on the left. Jerry Falwell's Moral Majority organization gave conservative Christians that chance. Though Falwell's organization and Pat Robertson's Christian Coalition would become marginalized over time, their political call to arms in the 1980s changed the face of the Republican Party and American politics.

GOP candidates running for positions ranging from local school boards to the U.S. Senate promised to roll back the cultural decay brought about by the most extreme influences of the 1960s. Republican candidates who convinced voters they would participate in a conservative counterrevolution were rewarded at the ballot box.

Soon enough, social issues began defining presidential campaigns. The personal morality and sex lives of Washington politicians became increasingly relevant. What was once the province of priests became the pastime for the press.

Even a candidate's personal religious views were subject to interrogation by the national press corp. Telling reporters to mind their own business was simply not an option anymore.

THE BORKING OF AMERICA

These cultural wars created a strange imbalance. Campaigns became focused on social issues that would account for less than 1 percent of most politicians' votes.

In my congressional career, I cast thousands of votes on a variety of issues. Yet I can recall no more than a handful of those votes concerning abortion, gay rights, or God. But those were the topics that newspapers and radio stations obsessed over.

The same press that claimed to be annoyed by having to cover social issues seemed drawn to them like a moth to a flame. During the 1980s, the cultural battle lines continued to harden, with attacks from both sides becoming more hyperbolic by the year. Those rabid political street fights sold newspapers and drove up TV ratings.

Predictably, the courts became the central focus of America's cultural wars. Judicial hearings on Supreme Court nominees soon became less focused on judicial temperament and legal training than on the nominees' positions on a few cultural issues. Since the Supreme Court's role shifted under Earl Warren and Warren Berger from interpreting the Constitution to legislating from the bench, issues like abortion predictably gained prominence and even preeminence in judicial confirmations.

The effect was to again distort hearings and make those battles primarily about issues that would occupy 1 percent of the Court's caseload.

America's judicial wars reached their nadir for conservatives when President Reagan nominated Robert Bork to the Supreme Court in 1987.

Judge Bork was widely considered to be one of the great conservative legal scholars of his generation, a man blessed with tremendous intellectual gifts, and a jurist respected by liberal and conservative colleagues alike. His record as a judge was unblemished. In a different era, Robert Bork's confirmation by the Senate would have been an afterthought.

But instead, Judge Bork turned out to be a bloodied political victim in America's increasingly nasty cultural war.

Less than an hour after Bork was nominated, Ted Kennedy, the most powerful liberal voice in America, delivered one of the most vitriolic speeches ever given by a senator about a Supreme Court nominee.

"Robert Bork's America," Kennedy began, "is a land in which women would be forced into back-alley abortions, blacks would sit at segregated lunch counters, rogue police could break down citizens' doors in midnight raids, and schoolchildren could not be taught about evolution."

Ted Kennedy's frantic attack was slander of a high order, but it performed the desired political trick. Judge Bork's nomination went down to defeat.

Yet this kind of tactic was not isolated to Robert Bork's nomination. As the *Wall Street Journal*'s Daniel Henninger wrote later, the Left's shabby treatment of conservative nominees actually began a year before Kennedy's attack against Bork, when Ronald Reagan nominated William Rehnquist to be Chief Justice of the United States.

Ted Kennedy and the Left tried to derail Rehnquist's nomination as well, not by making an issue of his 15-year record as an associate justice on the Supreme Court—there were simply no grounds for that—but instead by smearing him as a racist.

The Democratic attacks were based on claims that a younger Rehnquist had harassed black and Hispanic voters in the early 1960s. Kennedy's staff, for good measure, also dredged up a 1928 covenant on Rehnquist's home that restricted its conveyance to nonwhites. They also dug up his work product for a conservative justice who initially opposed the landmark case *Brown v. Board of Education*.

The Senate eventually confirmed Rehnquist. But blood was drawn.

Within five years, the Supreme Court would once again play a destructive role in America's culture wars. This time the Left tried to destroy the reputation of a conservative black justice with wild tales of porn stars and Coke cans.

Anita Hill's salacious testimony transfixed a nation and almost derailed Clarence Thomas's nomination.

A less cynical observer would have thought that liberals would celebrate the elevation of a qualified African American to the highest court in the land. But because Judge Thomas was a conservative, his nomination was met instead by a furious assault. The fact that Thomas was both black and a conservative made him a double threat.

In liberals' view, Clarence Thomas obviously didn't fit the ideological stereotype of a prominent African American. Since his ascendancy was seen as a challenge to their sacred political beliefs, Thomas's reputation would have to be destroyed.

Liberals would continue their assault on minority nominees during the Bush years.

It seems hard to believe all these years later that the effort to destroy Clarence Thomas was based on alleged off-color jokes told to Anita Hill—who, conservatives pointed out, continued to follow Thomas from job to job.

The moral outrage of the Left was especially ironic considering that Bill Clinton would become a beloved figure of the same feminist groups who lined the black justice up for a "high-tech lynching."

Feminist leaders like Betty Friedan declared that they simply didn't care if Bill Clinton was a sexual harasser or not.

Nina Burleigh, who covered the White House for *Time* magazine, candidly admitted to her feelings about President Clinton when she said, "I'd be happy to give him [oral sex] just to thank him for keeping abortion legal."

Their concern for Anita Hill was suddenly exposed as a farce.

Even Anita Hill herself said she was unconcerned with sexual harassment charges swirling around the Democratic president.

Because he seemed to represent so much of what conservatives hated about the 1960s, Bill Clinton's election to the White House fully engaged social conservatives. Mr. Clinton quickly confirmed their worst suspicions by pushing a series of social initiatives, from reversing pro-life policies to promoting military policies involving homosexuals to advancing restrictions on gun ownership to championing a greater intrusion by the federal government in education.

By the time the 1993 gay march on Washington came to an end, the Christian Right had been jolted into action.

A CULTURAL COLD WAR

Taken together, Bill Clinton's social policies in the early years of his presidency placed intense pressure on an existing fault line that would tear apart his moderate Democratic coalition.

In the 1994 midterm election, Republicans seized control of the House of Representatives for the first time in half a century by gaining 74 seats. It was the most significant political event of the decade, and it was driven in large measure by Republicans nationalizing the election by using cultural issues for political gain.

By the end of the decade, however, Republican efforts to impeach President Clinton backfired. The public may have been disgusted by Mr. Clinton's personal behavior, but it did not believe his failures warranted removal from office. President Clinton's cause was helped by a booming economy and by a correcting course the Democratic president made after the 1994 GOP landslide forced him back to the political middle.

The public hated the Lewinsky story, but many blamed Republicans for keeping it in the headlines. James Carville and the Clinton attack machine successfully portrayed independent counsel Ken Starr and the Republican Party as sex-obsessed buffoons. A majority of Americans agreed with a newly launched website called MoveOn.org that encouraged Congress to move past impeachment.

By the time Bill Clinton was out of office, both liberals and conservatives had suffered setbacks on moral issues. America's cultural wars had reached a stalemate.

The elections of George W. Bush in 2000 and 2004 would push that debate decidedly right, despite the closeness of those contests. Most important for Republicans, Mr. Bush placed two conservative justices on the Supreme Court. Bush had finally succeeded where every other Republican president since Eisenhower had failed, making the Supreme Court far more conservative than it was when he entered office.

John Roberts and Samuel Alito shifted the Court rightward as Republicans maintained a tight grip on the other branches as well. The fears that liberals had expressed to Tom Brokaw in *Boom* about how the Left's overreaching had empowered conservatives reached its most dramatic conclusion following the 2004 election.

While conservatives were dominating all three branches of government, something else of significance was taking place quietly out of sight: American culture undergoing the process of self-repair.

Even the conservative icon William J. Bennett began to reassess the conclusions of his landmark 1994 work *The Index of Leading Cultural Indicators,* which suggested that cultural decay threatened America's future. In 1994, Bennett ominously warned that "unless these exploding pathologies are reversed, they will lead to the decline and perhaps even to the fall of the American Republic."

Fifteen years later, Bennett would tell me on the set of *Morning Joe,* "We were wrong."

In fact, Bennett was not wrong. Had the social pathologies he wrote about not reversed themselves, American culture would have suffered grave consequences. But in one category after another, America's social indicators either stabilized or improved. Many of these social changes amounted to what could only be described as a "sea change."

Crime and welfare caseloads decreased dramatically, with the rates of both violent and property crime reaching their lowest levels since the early 1970s. The national welfare caseload dropped by more than 60 percent in the period since 1994.

Abortion rates and the overall number of abortions performed have decreased to levels not seen since the time of *Roe v. Wade.* Teen drug use and alcohol use have dropped substantially, as have teen pregnancies and teen sexual activity.

Education scores have risen, and the gap between minority students and white students has narrowed, while the rates of Americans graduating from high school and college have never been higher.

Bill Bennett rightly said the last decade proved once again that America had an amazing ability to learn from its mistakes and show the world its regenerative powers.

The reasons for that progress are varied; some of the explanations lie with changes in policy, while others are more attributable to shifts in attitudes. But it is accurate to say that conservatives' cultural counterrevolution succeeded beyond anyone's expectations, in large part because many Americans simply said "enough" to the nihilism of the 1960s.

America seems to be in the process of what social scientists refer to as moral "renorming." And while there are still battles to be fought, from local school board meetings to the halls of state legislatures to the chambers of the Supreme Court, the Left's ability to advance its social agenda in Washington has been blunted over the past quarter-century.

It remains to be seen whether Obama Democrats will dare tread the path that attempts to return Americans to the social radicalism of the 1960s.

So how should conservatives move forward in the Age of Obama?

As a general matter, liberals have used federal judges and Supreme Court justices to advance their cultural agenda. They do so for a simple reason: they can't win most cultural battles through a democratic process.

Because liberals have largely succeeded in nationalizing social issues through the courts, conservatives would be foolish to give up the fight when it comes to federal policies.

At the same time, conservatives should begin fighting to return these battles back to the states. Conservatives must recast the cultural debate in a fundamental way. By moving these battles away from Washington and back to local communities and states, they can return these debates over time back to where they belong.

This approach is commonly referred to as "federalism" or "constitutional conservatism." Whatever you want to call it, getting cultural battles out of Washington is a plea for greater self-government. It would also allow our federal government to focus on the goals of protecting our country, reviving our economy, and staying out of our personal lives.

It would also be constitutionally consistent with a movement that has long championed states' rights.

Let me explain.

Over the long run, constitutional conservatism has the best chance of advancing social conservatism. The advantage of federalism is that it allows issues like abortion and gay marriage to be decided by the will of the people instead of by nine men and women in black robes who possess no particular expertise on nonlegal issues. It will also keep issues in the states, where they belong—issues that our founding fathers never intended to be fought over in Congress or the courts.

Beyond that, constitutional conservatism would show conservatives' confidence in the intellectual and moral merits of their positions. If we believe abortion on demand is troubling or that same-sex unions would harm the institution of marriage, we should take those arguments to the people. If social conservatives' positions are democratically preferred, they will carry the day.

WE BLINDED THEM WITH SCIENCE

I happen to believe social conservatives *do* have the better arguments.

In recent years, it has become a political article of faith on the left that Republicans are "enemies of science." But it is the advancement of science and medical technology that is proving the greatest challenge to the champions of expansive abortion rights.

As with many of the social battles of the 1960s, the collective revulsion of American parents will eventually change this country's abortion-on-demand culture.

Here's why. Parents sitting through a three-dimensional ultrasound will find it harder to remain ambivalent on the issue of abortion as they view their unborn child in full detail.

How long would Americans tolerate abortion laws if CBS's *60 Minutes* ran the 3-D video of a single abortion procedure without comment or editing? Maybe a few weeks. Maybe a few days. Perhaps a few hours?

I realize that the chances of this happening are slim, since the overwhelming number of journalists I know support federalizing the issue of abortion. Nevertheless, imaging technology will only improve in the coming years, and these technological advancements will serve conservatives well.

Yet another scientific advancement will prove to be a political setback for abortion proponents. This is the medical miracle that saved my youngest son's life.

My wife, Susan, and I were surprised to learn last Christmas that we were going to have another child. The fact that she had a difficult pregnancy five years earlier caused us great concern from the moment we received the news.

Soon enough, Susan developed preeclampsia, which causes a pregnant woman's blood pressure to spike and her organs to shut down. Susan was hospitalized at the beginning of her seventh month. For weeks, high-risk doctors came in to weigh the risks to her health with that of the unborn baby's.

Since preeclampsia can lead to serious health problems or even death, we quickly became educated on the likelihood of survival for premature babies. Jack Scarborough was born 11 weeks early, but the remarkable scientific advances that saved his life also will serve pro-life advocates well in the future.

Over the last decade, scientific and medical advances in this field have been staggering, making successful births at earlier stages of the third trimester commonplace. As science and medicine move the viability of an unborn child into the second trimester, the moral and ethical arguments supporting abortion will become even more tenuous.

Science and technology will remain on the march, and conservatives will be the political beneficiaries of those changes and begin winning debates on the local level that they could never win in federal courts.

The same is true about same-sex marriage.

Gay marriage has been on the ballot 30 times—and it has always lost. While younger Americans are more accepting of same-sex unions, public sentiment on this issue still remains with traditional conservatives.

Most Americans believe that consenting adults' private sexual behavior is none of their business. But they also believe marriage should be restricted to one man and one woman. Far from being bigoted, those views are informed by tradition and history, by moral and religious beliefs, and by a traditional view of marriage's purpose. The conservative case against same-sex marriage can be summarized by what Russell Kirk once described as "the destruction of old patterns of life."

Personally, I am sympathetic to the traditionalist position. But no one has ever explained to me how two men getting married in a distant state threatens the strength of my marriage in Florida. Besides, many politicians who have been champions of marriage have probably done more damage to the institution in their personal lives than by the actions of two men a thousand miles away.

Again, I do not care to tell people in other parts of America how to conduct their personal lives. I do not see their deeply personal decisions as my business any more than the founding fathers saw it as their concern.

But the converse of that is true as well. If gays and lesbians try to tell me how my community in Florida should define marriage, I will resist those efforts in the name of constitutional conservatism.

There are other reasons conservatives should be strong advocates for federalism. It would, among other things, lead to a lessening of political tensions, since it would allow Americans to have a say in the outcome of hypersensitive cultural issues. The current model for resolving these wedge issues with nine judges only encourages voter anger.

One of the reasons abortion has been such a contentious issue for decades is that people understandably feel they have been disenfranchised. In his dissent in the 1992 case *Planned Parenthood of Southeastern Pennsylvania v. Casey,* Justice Antonin Scalia put it this way:

> The Court's description [in its majority opinion] of the place of *Roe* in the social history of the United States is unrecognizable. Not only did *Roe* not, as the Court suggests, *resolve* the deeply divisive issue of abortion; it did more than anything else to nourish it, by elevating it to the national level, where it is infinitely more difficult to resolve. National politics were not plagued by abortion protests, national abortion lobbying, or abortion marches on Congress before *Roe v. Wade* was decided. Profound disagreement existed among our citizens over the issue—as it does over other issues, such as the death penalty—but that disagreement was being worked out at the state level. As with many other issues, the division of sentiment within each State was not as closely balanced as it was among the population of the Nation as a

whole, meaning not only that more people would be satisfied with the results of state-by-state resolution, but also that those results would be more stable. Pre-*Roe*, moreover, political compromise was possible. *Roe*'s mandate for abortion on demand destroyed the compromises of the past, rendered compromise impossible for the future, and required the entire issue to be resolved uniformly, at the national level.

Allowing these issues to be settled in individual states won't completely drain them of acrimony, of course; we saw that with Proposition 8 in California, where gay rights advocates villified the Mormon Church and Pastor Rick Warren for opposing same-sex marriage. But allowing the public to have a say in the outcome of these debates will keep the temperature lower than it would otherwise be.

IT'S THE CONSTITUTION, STUPID

I would add another important element to this discussion. The governing charter of America, the Constitution, clearly guides us to resolving social issues on the state level.

The Constitution remains the guiding force in American history and public life. It is the document the president takes an oath to defend and uphold. And it is the document that has kept America united and free for more than two centuries. The architects of that Constitution—the wisest political minds since the philosophers of ancient Athens—believed in self-rule and created a system of checks and balances in order to prevent concentrated power.

It was never the intent of our founders to place social issues under the control of the centralized state. The Supreme Court's decision to do so in the 1960s and 1970s has led to the coarsening of political debate.

But any defense of federalism needs to acknowledge its limitations.

Deferring issues to the states, and even to a vote of the people, is not appropriate in every circumstance. The nation's first Republican, Abraham Lincoln, achieved fame and eventually a place on Mount Rushmore by opposing Stephen Douglas's argument on behalf of "popular sovereignty"—the belief that individual states should decide on slavery. Conservatives have not fully recovered from being on the wrong side of the civil rights struggle. They argued for "states' rights," which would have guaranteed the continuation of immoral, racist policies. So federalism is not an inviolate principle.

That said, the American system of government should possess a heavy bias toward constitutional conservatism. Unless the argument is overwhelmingly strong and involves a violation of basic constitutional rights, then conservative constitutionalism should carry the day. The burden of proof must be shifted back to those who seek to federalize social issues such as abortion and gay marriage.

Our position should be simple: Let people resolve moral issues in their communities. Not federal judges.

That doesn't mean that important moral issues won't make their way into politics; they will, and sometimes they should. But as a general matter, a member of Congress is better able to address issues of national defense and budget resolutions than he is able to address when meaningful life begins, when life should end, and exactly how marriage should be defined. I'm not convinced a Senate subcommittee is the place to determine whether a person is born gay or develops an attraction to members of the same sex over time.

WINNING BACK THE MIDDLE

My experience in Congress and as a member of the media has taught me that the public does not want to hear their national politicians debating divisive social issues. Whether one is pro-life or pro-choice, for or against same-sex marriage, such issues are uncomfortable subjects for most Americans to discuss.

Middle-class voters are consistently more concerned with their family's finances and our nation's defense than they are the philosophical debates surrounding the beginning of life or a same-sex union.

The party that is seen as being the "aggressor" on such social issues will continue to pay a price in national elections. I predict that American attitudes will only become more libertarian in the future.

Fairly or not, the perception among many voters that the GOP is too focused on social issues has had a devastating impact on Republican candidates in entire regions.

When I arrived in Congress in 1994, Maine had two Republican congressmen, New Hampshire had two, Connecticut had three, and Massachusetts had two.

Today, there are no Republican congressmen in all of New England. The perception that Republicans are obsessed over cultural issues helped turn one of the GOP's most loyal regions into a political killing field.

Conservatives will make gains in New England again when it returns to its constitutional heritage. Conservative politicians must once again let voters in every part of America know that limiting the reach of our centralized state is in everyone's best interest.

We should also make it clear to voters that our approach will defuse contentious social issues and remove them from Washington, whenever humanly possible.

Let liberals argue the opposite. Let them insist that their policies should be force-fed through federal fiat. Let them argue that Speaker Nancy Pelosi and liberal federal judges should micromanage moral issues from Maine to San Diego.

Conservatives will win that debate every time.

I am not just in sympathy with the goals of social conservatives; I *share* many of them. When I was a member of Congress, my prolife rating was consistently 100 percent. I supported the Defense of Marriage Act despite its stupid name, and I did so because it promoted constitutional conservatism and allowed states to make their own decisions on gay marriage. On Second Amendment issues, I consistently voted with the NRA.

I supported school choice, home schooling, and the right of local governments to display the Ten Commandments.

Fourteen years later, I stand by those votes. But certain moments in history require solutions that others do not. And in the political season we find ourselves in, it is time to remove moral battles in America's culture wars beyond the Beltway. That is the only way to protect the advances conservatives have made over the past generation.

It's essential as well that conservatives are careful in the tone and manner in which they make their case.

Social issues are inherently controversial and potentially explosive; it's therefore important that, if anything, we turn down the volume rather than turn it up. I say that as one who has too often come across as a fire-breathing advocate for the very issues I am now trying to remove from Washington's reach.

Not long ago a conservative-thought leader wrote this in *National Review:*

> Republicans need to move beyond the "culture war" model that worked well in the past. The rhetoric of candidates needs to be principled but civil, inviting rather than aggressive, and radiate grace instead of invoking apocalyptic warnings.

That sounds like a winning plan.

We should make our case for constitutional conservatism and all social issues in a way that is uplifting instead of angry. If we do, I believe conservatives will see in America what I witnessed at that town hall meeting in Florida: first silence, followed by scattered applause, followed by a healthy cheer.

I'd take that at this moment, and I think most other conservatives would as well.

6 MONEY CAN'T BUY ME LOVE

BUT IT CAN RENT THE WHITE HOUSE FOR FOUR YEARS

> Hypocrisy can afford to be magnificent in its promises, for never intending to go beyond promise, it costs nothing.
>
> —*Edmund Burke*

> If I am the Democratic nominee, I will aggressively pursue an agreement with the Republican nominee to preserve a publicly financed general election.
>
> —*Barack Obama*

One week before Barack Obama's historic White House win, the widely admired former Democratic senator Bob Kerrey was troubled.

The straight-talking Kerrey feared that the same Democrats who had spent their entire public life warning about money's corrosive impact on politics were being hypocritical by maintaining a conspiracy of silence over Mr. Obama's massive moneymaking machine.

Kerrey wrote, "We Democrats who strongly supported Sen.

Barack Obama's candidacy face an awkward fact: Either we are hypocrites for supporting limits to campaign spending, or we were wrong to support such limitations in the first place."

The former Nebraska senator helpfully defined a hypocrite as "a person who puts on a false appearance of virtue—who acts in contradiction to his or her stated beliefs or feelings. And that, it seems to me, is what we're doing now."

That's one way to put it.

Diogenes, with his lighted lantern, would have finally found in Bob Kerrey an honest man—a lonely Democratic leader willing to tell the truth about campaign financing.

As I have noted throughout this book, Republican lawmakers have been shameless hypocrites on the subject of limiting the size of government. But Democratic leaders have revealed themselves to be equally dishonest when the topic changes to campaign finance reform.

Anyone who believed otherwise had their faith shattered by the staggering amount of money raised and spent by Barack Obama in the 2008 presidential campaign.

Candidate Obama himself had badly misled the public on the subject in 2007, when he described himself as "a longtime advocate for public financing of campaigns."

It is true that when he was an underdog facing down the Clinton money machine, Mr. Obama believed public campaigns "combined with free television and radio time are a way to reduce the influence of moneyed special interests."

But that was only his position until it was in his political interest to break the campaign promise that was central to his identity as a crusading politician of change. But once it became necessary for his political advancement, Senator Obama quickly tossed aside public dollars, disregarded decades of Democratic dogma, and raked in obscene amounts of cash for his campaign coffers.

The Democrats' candidate of change had come a long way from when he called money "the original sin" of Washington.

Suddenly, Obama adopted the belief that money was not only *not* sinful, but manna from the political heavens. Suddenly the great reformer sounded an awful lot like old-time party bosses who famously called campaign cash the mother's milk of American politics.

Instead of changing the way political campaigns were run, the candidate of change decided instead to change his position. Thankfully for him, a compliant press remained silent on his shameless conversion.

Even as Senator Obama was raising and spending record amounts to crush the Clinton machine in Democratic primaries, he kept promising to "preserve a publicly financed general election" in the general election. To his credit, Barack Obama faithfully continued to support campaign finance limits . . . right up until the moment he didn't.

Under campaign finance rules, candidates have the option of accepting $85 million in tax dollars for the fall general election campaign. But in return, that $85 million is all they are allowed to spend between their party convention and Election Day. The system was created to keep a level playing field in presidential politics and stop one candidate from buying an election.

For Democrats, public financing of campaigns had always been one of their greatest articles of faith, the very embodiment of "good government." Accepting public financing was the only way to ensure that a candidate could not pave his way to the White House on a road of campaign cash.

Democrats like Barack Obama had long argued that public financing, along with free television time, was the only way to make sure that a campaign would be decided on the issues instead of by campaign cash's "corrupting" influence.

No presidential candidate had ever rejected public financing since Congress put the system in place in the 1970s. There was no reason to believe the first candidate to do so would be a liberal Democrat who had long claimed to be a champion of that very public financing system.

THE CANDIDATE OF CHANGE . . . CHANGES HIS MIND

Throughout the first half of 2008, John McCain and Barack Obama both vowed to live by the rules of public financing. But when breaking that promise became the expedient thing to do, Mr. Obama broke his word.

The cause of public financing soon found itself thrown under the same bus that Barack Obama rolled over Jeremiah Wright, his church, Tom Daschle, and any person, place, or thing that stood in the way of Mr. Obama's advancement.

Why would the Democratic candidate turn his back on what party leaders had considered to be the Holy Grail of clean campaigning? The answer is depressingly simple. Barack Obama concluded he could kill McCain's White House hopes with hundreds of millions of dollars in cold, hard cash. And he was right.

When it became clear to Senator Obama that he could raise and spend more money by forgoing free government funds than by accepting them, he calculated that it would help him far more to go back on his word than to stand by his former principles. Again, his political calculus was correct.

The elections of 2000 and 2004 shattered every previous fundraising record. But Mr. Obama obliterated both records set by those money-rich campaigns. In fact, Barack Obama spent more campaign cash than George W. Bush and John Kerry *combined.*

In August 2008, Barack Obama hauled in a staggering $66 million in campaign cash. That was a *one-month* fundraising record. In September of that same year, the Obama money machine raked in $150 million! That level of cash flooding into a campaign was simply beyond compare.

One wonders what stories the media would have written had a Republican set those records.

Because of his decision to opt out of the same public financing system that he once championed, Senator Obama was able to raise more than $639 million in campaign cash.

It turns out that Obama was right both before and after he changed his tune on public financing of campaigns.

Big money *does* buy elections, and going back on his word *was* in his best political interest. That's because $639 million bought the Democratic nominee an unprecedented political advantage and, eventually, the title "President of the United States."

That $639 million meant that Barack Obama outspent John McCain by a quarter of a billion dollars. That shocking differential was unprecedented in American history and created an advantage impossible for Mr. McCain to overcome.

Barack Obama outspent John McCain by $250,000,000.00!

What did that quarter-of-a-billion-dollar advantage mean in practical terms? Barack Obama's total cash haul of $639 million meant the Democratic political operation had thousands more boots on the ground to push the Obama machine's campaign agenda.

In Pennsylvania, that machine set up 83 field offices, compared with McCain's 30. In Colorado, it was 59 to McCain's 13; in Virginia, 51 to 19. Obama's $639 million built a bigger political operation, hired more staff, sent more mail, hired more phone banks, made more robocalls, and funded a massive get-out-the-vote effort. And, in the end, bought more votes.

In Florida, the Obama machine spent $40 million to McCain's paltry $13 million. Anyone who has ever worked in Florida politics knows that kind of money advantage bought Barack Obama Florida's 27 electoral votes. No statewide candidate running in

Florida has ever overcome that kind of financial discrepancy. Ever.

The $639 million war chest also meant that the Obama machine could campaign in battleground states in a way that Al Gore and John Kerry never could.

The Obama machine outspent McCain in Indiana by roughly 7 to 1, in Virginia by 4 to 1, in Ohio by 2 to 1, and in North Carolina by 3 to 2.

The $639 million war chest also meant that the Obama machine could flood swing states with the lowest common denominator of political advertising: the 30-second TV ad.

Barack Obama spent more than four times what McCain spent on campaign commercials. He had a 3-to-2 advantage on network TV buys. In some markets, Obama bought up all the available media slots, so that McCain couldn't respond even if he wanted to do so.

In one October weekend during the campaign's homestretch, the Obama money machine helped its candidate outspend John McCain by a ratio of 200 to 1 in the key battleground state of Virginia.

It is hard to imagine how *any* candidate who bought that kind of ad blitz could do anything *but* win.

A LOW ROAD TO VICTORY PAVED WITH POSITIVE PRESS

Obama's dollar-over-dollar advertising advantage also allowed him to shape and dominate the political conversation. And more often than not, the candidate of change ran 30-second attack ads that were predictably negative and employed grainy images of McCain while exaggerating claims about his positions.

One heavy-rotation attack ad claimed that John McCain put "bad actors ahead of taxpayers" for supporting the October financial bailout that Barack Obama also supported.

Another that drew political blood and twisted the truth claimed that John McCain wanted to tax health care benefits. While the claim contained a grain of truth, it distorted the facts, since McCain also provided an even larger tax break for health care benefits to those same voters.

But as is usual in negative 30-second spots, voters get only a distorted view of the facts.

Since John McCain kept his earlier promise and stayed within the public financing system, he couldn't respond to Barack Obama's sleazy campaign tactics.

The lies about McCain's health care program stuck. Soon, Barack Obama, unlike most Democratic general election candidates before him, led in polls on the question of which candidate could be more trusted on taxes.

In one of the more ironic turns of the campaign, the same candidate who was airing more attack ads than any other politician in the history of U.S. politics was simultaneously being praised in the press as a new kind of leader.

Most in the media remained mute on this issue and refused to run stories that would educate voters as to how large a role big money and negative ads played in Barack Obama's campaign.

"The American people aren't looking for someone who can divide this country—they're looking for someone who will lead this country," the Democratic nominee said.

"They can run misleading ads and pursue the politics of anything goes, but it's not going to work. Not this time"—so said the man who ran more negative ads than any politician in the history of America.

That he could say it with a straight face made his statement that much more disconcerting.

To this day, I remain embarrassed by the mainstream media's failure to report on the biggest story of the 2008 campaign.

How exactly did a presidential front-runner who ran the most

negative advertising assault in American history get away with
shamelessly claiming the moral high ground on the issue of negative campaigning? The only answer is that a compliant press proved
themselves to be as hypocritical as Bob Kerrey's Democrats.

If you question my conclusions on President Obama's slash-
and-burn TV campaign, look at the objective numbers.

The Campaign Media Analysis Group recently reported that
Barack Obama ran 119,101 negative ads costing more than $65 mil-
lion in the final stretch of the campaign.

Mr. Obama ran $30 million *more* in negative ads than McCain's
entire advertising budget over the same period.

During one week alone in October, Barack Obama spent more
than $22 million for 37,000 negative ads. Obama's $22 million of
attack ads over that one week was almost three times the amount
McCain spent on such ads in the entire campaign, and more than
twice the amount the Obama machine spent on positive ads that
laid out his agenda.

Barack Obama's $639 million money pot also meant that he
could air a half-hour prime-time infomercial that briefly delayed
the start of Game Six of the World Series. His prime-time ad aired
on three networks with a price tag that reached into the millions.

Mr. Obama's $639 million money machine also meant he could
even advertise in video games like Guitar Hero.

As *The Onion,* a satirical newspaper, joked, the Obama campaign even bought ad space on the side of the Straight Talk
Express.

Senator Obama's $639 million also meant that his political orga-
nization could outspend Senator McCain by $100 million in the
final week of the campaign. That staggering last-minute money
advantage helped push the Democratic candidate's margin of victory beyond most polling expectations.

In short, Barack Obama's decision to opt out of public financing
meant that cash influenced the outcome of the 2008 presidential

campaign in a way that it had never influenced politics before. By any traditional campaign standard, Senator Obama bought a one-way ticket to the White House.

Not surprisingly, the very people who devoted their entire careers to limiting the influence of money on politics didn't whisper a word of protest about the victory that their candidate bought with unprecedented amounts of cash. In fact, they seemed intoxicated by it.

Can you imagine what these liberal "reformers" would have said had George W. Bush and Dick Cheney held such an advantage over John Kerry just four years earlier?

Bob Kerrey was right. All those campaign finance crusaders were revealed in 2008 as nothing more than partisan hypocrites.

Outside of Bob Kerrey and a few other lonely souls, Barack Obama's cash-soaked political machine didn't faze Democratic bosses.

Many justified their two-faced view of campaign financing by arguing implausibly that Mr. Obama had built a "parallel public financing system" that relied on millions of small donors. Many apologists also suggested that his moneymaking machine was making America more democratic.

It was a frantic effort to spin an embarrassing situation. Too bad it wasn't true. In the end, most of Barack Obama's contributions came from rich people.

OBAMA: THE FAT CATS' MEOW

Almost 75 percent of Barack Obama's campaign funds came from large donors, who opened their wallets for $200 and above.

Nearly half of the "reform" candidate's dollars came from wealthy donors who gave $1,000 or more.

While the Obama team also drew in small donors, the reality is that Barack Obama raised more money in $200-plus amounts than any presidential candidate in history raised in total contributions of any size.

This supposed champion of small campaign donors also raised *twice* as much money in checks of $1,000 or more than any previous candidate in U.S. history.

And if every small contribution somehow evaporated, Mr. Obama would *still* have raked in more campaign cash than any candidate before him—and by a very large margin.

The truth is that Reformer Obama's pot of campaign cash was filled by those "moneyed special interests" that the candidate of change once found so objectionable.

In his September haul, more than 600 people wrote checks of $25,000 or more to the so-called Obama Victory Fund.

These objective facts confirm the following realities in U.S. politics:

1. The campaign finance reform community is filled with hypocrites who are not burdened by feelings of shame.

2. Barack Obama was for keeping big money out of politics before he was against it.

3. The 2008 election was more greatly influenced by money than any campaign before it.

And to all three realities, I offer the same response.
So what?

Conservatives should celebrate Barack Obama's shamelessness, if for no other reason than that he renounced a taxpayer subsidy. He ended up doing the right thing for the wrong reasons. Since we don't need one more politician on the dole, I hope conservative candidates follow Mr. Obama's lead in the future.

Many conservatives believed the 2008 fundraising story was a moment of poetic justice for John McCain, who found out too late that the campaign finance system he created was an albatross that destroyed his presidential hopes.

It is true that the same rules that applied to John McCain also applied to Barack Obama. But Obama's plan to stand on principle quickly changed when he saw the pot of money at the end of his political rainbow.

As the man who established the campaign finance system, John McCain simply could make the same shameless political somersaults that Barack Obama did.

While the financing of Senator Obama's victory should have chiseled the epitaph on the tombstone of the existing finance system, it predictably has not.

Democrats claim that campaign finance reform is even more a matter of high moral principle now that President Obama is in the White House. They say that the president was forced to opt out of public financing because the current scheme is "broken," and they want to pile even more limits and regulations on top of the ones that have already failed.

"I am firmly committed to reforming the system, so that it's viable in today's campaign climate," Obama said recently, again with a straight face. That he would even dare broach the subject again suggests something deeply troubling about his political character.

With President Obama and his Chicago campaign machine, power politics means never having to say you're sorry.

Burned by John McCain's fundraising weakness, many Republicans joined Democrats behind the scenes to work up a new campaign finance regime. Claiming equally high moral principle, Republicans suddenly became filled with the audacity of hope that they could pry the money weapon out of President Obama's hands before 2012.

One political poll after another suggests that rank-and-file Americans don't care much about campaign finance. The complex

web of regulations and rules primarily affect the rich and powerful, political insiders, Washington lobbyists, and other suspect
classes. Perhaps that is why the subject holds little interest for most
voters.

But more voters should care.

Many conservatives believe that campaign finance rules are undermining our most basic freedoms, including our First Amendment right to engage in free speech and to participate in the
political process.

George F. Will, a conservative intellectual who has written
more authoritatively on this topic than anyone else, has flatly
declared:

> Nothing in American history—not the Left's recent campus
> "speech codes," not the right's depredations during the 1950s
> McCarthyism or the 1920s "red scare," not the Alien and
> Sedition Acts of the 1790s—matches the menace to the First
> Amendment posed by campaign "reforms" advancing under
> the protective coloration of political hygiene.

To show how suffocating these political speech codes have
become, look at the example of NASCAR driver Kirk Shelmerdine, who in 2004 put a "Bush-Cheney" bumper sticker on his
race car. The driver was immediately fined by the federal government for making an unreported campaign expenditure.

You read that right: a NASCAR driver was busted by Big
Brother for a single bumper sticker.

Sadly, stupid cases like Shelmerdine's are not the exception, but
too often the rule.

Once considered the most sacrosanct form of speech under the
U.S. Constitution, political speech now enjoys less constitutional
protection than some forms of pornography.

BIG MONEY, SMALL POTATOES

If the 2008 campaign taught us anything, it is that campaign finance reform is driven by partisanship and not principle.

One would think that Republicans interested in returning to conservative principles would challenge the status quo of campaign finance codes. But true to form, many GOP members are more focused on regaining power than standing on principle. They are predictably galloping in the opposite direction.

So how big of a problem is money in campaigns? Is our system so "awash in money" that it risks a crippling degree of corruption?

George Will dismissed the "crisis" as small potatoes.

He noted that the Center for Responsive Politics calculated that $2.4 billion was spent on presidential campaigns in the two-year election cycle that began in January 2007, and an additional $2.9 billion was spent on 435 House and 35 Senate contests.

Will concluded that the amount spent on such political contests was not a threat to democracy, since the $5.3 billion spent on those campaigns was a billion dollars less than Americans spent over the same time period on potato chips.

George Will and other Americans can be excused for asking whether our democratic system is really so fragile that it can't withstand the same level of advertising that Americans lavish on corn chips and salsa.

God help us if it is.

The modern era of campaign finance reform has its origins in the late 1960s.

As Lyndon Johnson's big-government liberalism was losing its popularity with political contributors, Democrats decided something needed to be done to foil a growing Republican insurgency. Since the GOP was seen as the party of "Big Money" and enjoyed a marginal fundraising advantage in presidential contests, campaign laws limiting fundraising seemed like a shrewd scheme for Democrats.

The effort gathered steam after Richard Nixon won the White House in 1968.

Facing another Nixon-sponsored defeat the next year, the Democratic Congress passed the Federal Election Campaign Act in 1971, which severely limited any expenditure that might "influence" an election.

Not surprisingly, political activities that preserved Democratic advantages in the area of union efforts and big-city ward heeling were protected under the Campaign Act.

In the 1976 U.S. Supreme Court decision *Buckley v. Valeo,* the Court struck down parts of the 1971 act on First Amendment grounds. The Supreme Court concluded that limiting contributions to noncandidate political organizations like those supporting abortion and gun rights was unconstitutional.

From that moment forward, groups like the NRA were exempt from the Court's scrutiny unless they engaged in political activity that was "unambiguously related" to a political race. For example, if these groups specifically called for the election or defeat of a candidate, they then became subject to spending limits.

Still, the high court kept in place the 1971 public financing scheme and the limits on what individuals could give to political candidates.

Good-government reformers took another whack at campaign finance reform early in the Bush administration.

Their efforts led to the passage of the McCain-Feingold reforms in 2002. Named after its sponsors, Democrat Russ Feingold of Wisconsin and John McCain, the bill passed in the wake of several fundraising scandals that erupted during the Clinton administration.

McCain-Feingold banned unlimited "soft money" contributions that fund party-building activities and political-issue ads that don't specifically support a candidate. It also restricted the ability of groups like the NRA and NARAL to broadcast ads that name a candidate within 60 days of an election.

Why did a campaign bill that squelched free speech pass so easily through a GOP Congress and get signed by a Republican president?

One factor that drove conservative members to supporting McCain-Feingold was the fact that Bill Clinton's White House seemed to be caught in a constant blizzard of fundraising scandals throughout the 1990s. Some conservatives were frustrated by Mr. Clinton's continued ability to skirt existing laws and hoped that new regulations would discourage such bad behavior in the future.

Other conservatives were as indifferent as the general public on the issue of campaign finance reform. It was easy for these members to vote for a set of reforms that many saw as meaningless.

And others realized that McCain-Feingold was like an incumbent-protection act.

Republicans had a reason to support the reforms because they would no longer be vulnerable to political hit jobs in the final days of their campaigns by negative union ads. Democrats, likewise, would no longer have to worry about a late spending spree by the NRA or pro-life groups.

Five years later, the Supreme Court pared down some of McCain-Feingold's excesses. But the high court didn't go far enough.

While I admit I am less concerned with campaign finance reform's chilling effects on the First Amendment than I am with speech codes on college campuses and in the media, I still support the Court overturning McCain-Feingold and other campaign finance schemes that limit political involvement.

The First Amendment exists in part to protect the rights of citizens to speak freely, which includes the ability to criticize their government.

McCain-Feingold chills free speech and the ability to criticize the president, would-be presidents, and members of Congress by the groups that have the megaphones to make those criticisms heard: political parties and political advocacy groups on all sides.

CENSORSHIP? WHAT CENSORSHIP?

Campaign finance reformers are fond of saying that money is not speech. But this proposition rests on the fiction that political money can be regulated without regulating political speech.

That argument is as specious as government claiming it was not in the business of banning books all the while it censored content within the books' covers.

It is a distinction without a difference.

Instead of censoring speech, Democrats should instead embrace the words of a liberal icon, former Supreme Court justice William O. Douglas, who said:

> It usually costs money to communicate an idea to a large audience. But no one would seriously contend that a limitation on the expenditure of money to print a newspaper would not deprive the publisher of freedom of the press. Nor can the fact that it costs money to make a speech—whether it be hiring a hall or purchasing time on the air—make the speech any the less an exercise of First Amendment rights.

A far less liberal Supreme Court justice, Clarence Thomas, also put it well: "There is no constitutionally significant distinction between campaign contributions and expenditures. Both forms of speech are central to the First Amendment."

Simply put, an attack on the funding of speech is an attack on speech itself; and by attacking a candidate's ability to fund her campaign's message, the government is attacking her ability to engage in political speech in the manner she finds most effective.

Another argument for campaign finance reform has been that it will end the "appearance" of "corruption." The argument suggests that legislative votes are solely determined by campaign contributions. But it is not that simple.

Having served in Congress, I know that many factors influence how a legislator votes, from party affiliation to ideology to public opinion to core convictions.

A good example of how money plays a less significant role in politics than many think is my relationship with the NRA.

In my first campaign, members of the guns rights group preferred my opponent so much that they spread lies about me in campaign fliers. After winning, I told the NRA lobbyist that despite the fact that political operatives in his organization behaved like political thugs, I would be their most reliable vote. But I had a bit of advice for the NRA lobbyist.

"Keep your money. I didn't need it before, and I sure don't need it now."

I went on to tell the lobbyist I would never do a favor for any group that sanctioned such dishonest attacks against me. I got up and left the breakfast not expecting to speak with the group again.

The NRA gave me the maximum contribution allowed by law throughout my political career—not because they thought I would carry water for them on the Hill, but because they knew I would never vote against the interests of the Second Amendment.

Politicians' votes may follow political contributions, but it is also true that people make contributions to political leaders who are naturally inclined to fight on behalf of issues they care about.

During an oral argument in February 2006, Chief Justice John Roberts asked the Vermont attorney general, "How many prosecutions for political corruption have you brought?" The answer was none.

Roberts then asked the Vermont attorney general if political corruption in Vermont was a serious problem.

The attorney general answered, "It is."

When Roberts asked him for an example to support his claim that campaign contributions from Vermont interest groups "often determine what positions candidates and officials take on issues," the AG couldn't offer a single example.

Those who say, as former senator Bill Bradley has, that their goal is to "totally take special interests out of our election process" are attempting to silence people who have every right to express their opinions and views during an election.

One person's "special interest lobbyist" may be another's champion for freedom. Besides, who is Bill Bradley, or anyone, to determine who should be silenced and who should not?

Senator Bradley is a good man, but he can't make that judgment and he shouldn't try.

Another result of campaign finance limits is to increase the influence of the media on election outcomes. After all, diminishing the influence of American citizens who can publicly fight for a candidate or cause only serves to strengthen the influence of the mainstream media.

As a member of the press, I have seen up close throughout the 2008 presidential campaign that increasing the power and influence of the media in U.S. elections is not always the wisest path to take.

Every reputable media research organization that studied the 2008 presidential race was able to quantify a clear media bias favoring Barack Obama over John McCain, and the degree of that bias was depressing to anyone who longs for a vibrant, unbiased press.

One other point about "reforms" passed by politicians for politicians: whether the issue involves campaign cash, ethics reforms, or term limits, I learned quickly in Congress that the party in power always skews the rules to try to stay in power.

So if Democrats control Congress, you can bet any reform bill will have a disproportionately negative impact on groups like the NRA and National Right to Life.

If Republicans pass legislation in the future, you can expect that legislation to limit the power of unions and left-wing advocacy groups.

In the words of Earth, Wind and Fire, "That's the way of the world."

THE MILLIONAIRE MADE ME DO IT

In a 2003 Supreme Court dissent, Justice Antonin Scalia wrote, "The present legislation targets for prohibition certain categories of campaign speech that are particularly harmful to incumbents." He continued,

> Is it accidental, do you think, that incumbents raise about three times as much "hard money"—the sort of funding generally not restricted by this legislation—as do their challengers? . . . Or that lobbyists (who seek the favor of incumbents) give 92 percent of their money in "hard" contributions? . . . Is it an oversight, do you suppose, that the so-called "millionaire provisions" raise the contribution limit for a candidate running against an individual who devotes to the campaign (as challengers often do) great personal wealth, but do not raise the limit for a candidate running against an individual who devotes to the campaign (as incumbents often do) a massive election "war chest"?

Scalia concluded that campaign finance is designed to assist "flush-with-hard-money incumbents" and to hurt "cash-strapped challengers."

The "millionaire provisions" that Scalia mentioned exposed the fraudulence of the entire scam.

Supposedly to "level the playing field" between wealthy and nonwealthy candidates, the rules saddled self-financing candidates with burdens designed to help their opponents. When such a well-to-do contender exceeded a particular personal spending threshold, his opponent could receive triple the per-election limit of $2,300 from each donor.

But if receiving more than $2,300 corrupts a politician, as the general rules imply, why doesn't $6,900 corrupt those politicians when they are running against a millionaire? And for that matter, why aren't the millionaires corrupted by how they made their own money?

It doesn't take a very creative mind to realize that politicians of modest means will almost always support laws like the "millionaire provision" because they fear being threatened politically by rich challengers. And while that is understandable, it is philosophically inconsistent and constitutionally dubious. Either the arbitrary amount of $2,300 is the most a candidate can accept without falling victim to political bribery or it is not.

The suggestion that a millionaire's opponent suddenly becomes three times as virtuous as a result of running against a rich opponent is ridiculous.

In a victory for free speech and intellectual consistency, the Supreme Court overturned the millionaire's amendment in 2008. But the case again exposed the absurdity of the campaign finance charade.

Campaign finance advocates continue to support contribution limits because they say they purge those politicians who lack a broad base of support. And yet candidates with huge personal fortunes, like Mayor Michael Bloomberg of New York, usually overwhelm their opponents, who are hobbled by those very donation limits.

In 2005, the Senate included four members, all Democrats, whose fortune exceeded $100 million, a dozen whose fortunes exceeded

$10 million, and at least 30 members of the House who were worth $5 million or more.

The way to ensure that politics does not become the exclusive domain of rich Americans is not by increasing limits on political speech, but rather by eliminating them.

CLEAN FOR GENE

Not so long ago, an ambitious politician could mount a national campaign with the help of a few well-heeled backers.

In 1968, Stewart Mott, an eccentric millionaire known for promoting liberal causes, bankrolled the candidacy of Senator Eugene McCarthy for the Democratic nomination.

Mott didn't give to McCarthy so he could secure special favors or buy an "in the pocket" senator. Rather, he wanted the Democrats to be a more dovish party toward Vietnam. He believed that McCarthy was the best advocate to advance his ideals.

Few believed that "Clean Gene" was a Manchurian candidate doing the bidding of Mott. It was the other way around: Mott supported McCarthy because he approved of his ideas. Their partnership was mutually beneficial and added a needed and eloquent voice to the political debate in 1968.

That year, almost everyone knew where McCarthy was getting his money; the public was left to draw its own conclusions about the senator's motivations. The realities of that campaign demonstrated a certain confidence in the public and its maturity.

We should invest that level of confidence in voters in our time as well.

Like Gene McCarthy, Teddy Roosevelt and Franklin Roosevelt both had their campaigns financed by multimillionaires. That support allowed both political giants to reach the White House and transform American politics in their era.

If McCarthy, Teddy Roosevelt, or FDR had to run for office in the twenty-first century, they would spend far less time campaigning across America and far greater periods locked inside a room scanning call lists to find thousands of rich people to contribute a few thousand dollars to their campaign.

Contributors like Stewart Mott could only advance their views in the modern era of American politics by running for office themselves. And a middle-class candidate who hoped to challenge Michael Bloomberg in New York or Barack Obama in the next presidential election would have to do so by staying on the phone for month after month after month, trying to accumulate the massive amounts of money that both Bloomberg and Obama can now generate in the blink of an eye.

That is no way to run a political system. But it is a good way to rig one.

Campaign finance has only made American politics less competitive. The complex set of rules has not expanded participation, the number of challengers elected, or the fairness of the overall process.

Donation limits have only served to drive good men and women out of politics. Without a Mott or a Medici to underwrite their campaigns, politicians will spend too much of their campaign raising campaign cash.

Campaign finance has also made the political process less transparent. More often than not, political supporters who give the maximum contribution to their favorite candidate will become more creative in funneling additional money their way. Members of Congress with whom I served joked about how their campaign coffers were often filled with donations from hunting dogs or preschool children.

Too often, I have seen the campaign finance shell game also played out on the state and local levels.

DAFFY FOR OBAMA

Barack Obama's own record-breaking campaign received contributions from dubious sources like Doodad Pro, Bart Simpson, King Kong, Daffy Duck, and Mr. Good Will.

Hillary Clinton's campaign received similar contributions during the Democratic primary. But their campaigns were not exceptions to the rule. Instead, they were simply the campaigns whose questionable contributions received the biggest headlines.

But the rich and powerful have also started using the rules of McCain-Feingold to shift their money to independent groups that are harder to trace, like the "527" groups that can work to crush a candidate's campaign.

The irony is that campaign finance reforms that were sold in the name of minimizing the influence of "fat cats" have made one of the world's richest men among the most powerful in politics.

George Soros, the billionaire hedge fund manager turned left-wing activist, operates a fleet of liberal 527s so broad that it is nearly untraceable. Soros is a huge donor to the liberal group MoveOn.org, which ran a full-page ad in the *New York Times* attacking an American war hero ("General Petraeus or General Betray Us? Cooking the Books for the White House").

Other groups favoring Republicans popped up too, like the Swift Boat Veterans for Truth in 2004. Once again, the road to hell is paved with good intentions and campaign finance regulations.

As is usually the case with efforts to reform campaign spending, the cure ends up being worse than the underlying disease.

In many ways, the newer system of outside groups is more corrupting than the way things used to be run, because today accountability for nasty ad campaigns can be shifted from individual candidates to special-interest groups. That makes it even more difficult for voters to follow the money and judge the indebtedness of candidates to anonymous donors or to these special-interest groups.

It also promotes the illusion that such influence no longer exists in politics, when that is simply not true.

"The dam is broken," McCain helplessly observed after Barack Obama opted out of public financing, and he was right.

Former FEC chairman Bradley Smith said of the 2008 campaign, "Obama's epic fundraising should put to rest all the shibboleths about campaign finance reform—that it is needed to prevent corruption, that it equalizes the playing field, or that tax subsidies are needed to prevent corruption."

Mr. Bradley probably also knows that no presidential candidate will ever again put himself in the hapless position that John McCain did in 2008, as his opponent was outspending him in TV ads at a ratio that sometimes approached 200 to 1.

Today, many of the same liberals who have denied that money buys protected political speech may be forced to admit that their contributions to President Obama were, in fact, a form of political expression. Or they could just adopt Bob Kerrey's position and admit that they are hypocrites who will exchange their personal values for political power.

Speaking of hypocrisy, some Republicans are now sanctimoniously adopting positions once held by these same Democrats.

In Washington, you can always bet that the party outspent by the other will start working the day after the election to shift the rules of the political game to disrupt an opponent's advantage.

TRUST BUT VERIFY

But conservatives, and all Americans, would be best served by removing the campaign finance restrictions on fundraising altogether, rather than limiting the speech of Americans who want to be involved in American politics.

If Michael Bloomberg can contribute millions of dollars to

his own campaign, why can't candidates like Gene McCarthy or Franklin Roosevelt receive that level of support from other Americans?

What would happen if my approach were adapted? Well, it would look a lot like Barack Obama's 2008 campaign, where Americans' free-speech rights weren't impeded by "good-government" reformers like Barack Obama himself.

While President Obama's most shameless political move in the 2008 campaign may have been his decision to opt out of the public financing system, it was also his shrewdest.

More than any other thing he did or said, Barack Obama turning his back on almost 40 years of Democratic dogma virtually ensured his election as president. And the model the new president put together over the course of his campaign should actually cheer conservatives who oppose campaign finance reforms.

Barack Obama may have shown us the way to the future.

Thanks, Mr. President.

Currently, the American people have the cost-free and voluntary option of checking off a box on their income tax returns that donates $1 to the public financing of campaigns. Participation peaked at 28.7 percent in 1980; today, it has dropped to less than 10 percent.

In his dam-is-broken comments, McCain warned darkly, "We're now going to see huge amounts of money coming into political campaigns."

Perhaps Senator McCain is right about this too, but the great war hero should not assume that it is a bad thing for Americans to spend at least as much money on electing a president and Congress as they do on buying potato chips.

It is time to trust the American people and remove limits on how much an individual can donate to a campaign.

As Justice Scalia once put it,

The premise of the First Amendment is that the American people are neither sheep nor fools, and hence fully capable of considering both the substance of speech presented to them and its proximate and ultimate source. If that premise is wrong, our democracy has a much greater problem to overcome than merely the influence of amassed wealth.

The key to such a system functioning effectively is transparency.

While it is important for conservatives to fight for an elimination of spending limits, it is just as critical to create the greatest transparency in the history of political fundraising.

Office seekers should be allowed to raise whatever amount they can from whomever they want. But they should then be required to scan the contribution check and immediately post it on the Internet, along with their supporter's full name, address, and place of employment.

Technology is a very powerful tool.

It should be employed to require candidates to post all donations in an online database in real time every 24 hours, instead of the monthly or quarterly reporting that is required at present. A searchable record that also highlights trends and statistics would give voters the option of determining for themselves whether candidates are getting too much money from unsavory or undesirable sources.

It would also make politicians more cautious about accepting such checks, especially if they're about to vote on subsidies for a big industry that pours dollars into their account right before the vote.

The controversy about questionable contributions would be in real time, and political behavior would be altered. Journalists would be able to use the unprecedented transparency afforded by such a system to immediately sniff out corruption and deals that seem to spawn quid pro quos.

Maybe it would even encourage the political class, especially conservatives, to build on President Obama's fundraising model.

If members of the conservative movement want to regain control of the White House, they need to study how Barack Obama, through an act of jaw-dropping cynicism, got so many Americans interested in contributing money to his cause.

Without artificially set limits, a little-known candidate who is willing to fight for smaller government and taxpayers' rights could inspire a handful of donors who wanted a little more from their government than what the U.S. Constitution promised.

And who knows, if conservatives in Washington start acting conservative again, maybe millions of other Americans would want to contribute to their cause as well.

7 DEATH BY ENTITLEMENT

IT'S NOT ABOUT IDEOLOGY.
IT'S ABOUT MATH.

I am a firm believer in the people. If given the truth, they can be depended upon to meet any national crises. The great point is to bring them the real facts.

—Abraham Lincoln

Facts do not cease to exist because they are ignored.

—Aldous Huxley

It is becoming more difficult by the day to be an optimist—especially if you consider yourself to be an economic conservative.

That's because Barack Obama's fiscal policy since entering the White House can only be described as radical.

The Democratic president's stimulus package was the biggest spending bill in U.S. history. It amounted to 5 percent of America's GDP. The New Deal was only 2 percent.

After passing the stimulus package, President Obama quickly announced plans to spend double the New Deal's percentage to pay for the nationalization of health care. If the president succeeds at that mission, his federal government will gain control over another one-sixth of the American economy.

The president also announced his intention to spend six times the amount of that health care "investment" on his first budget. If the Senate budget chairman and the Congressional Budget Office are to be believed, Obama's almost $4 trillion budget will cripple the U.S. economy.

The American president's fiscal policies are, in fact, so extreme that even the French and German governments have angrily pushed back on suggestions that they follow Barack Obama's reckless approach.

The current European Union president even called the president's economic agenda the "road to hell."

But European leaders aren't the only ones expressing concerns.

The Chinese government is now suggesting that their government will move away from the U.S. dollar if Obama Democrats don't start showing more fiscal restraint.

In the midst of such bleak news, conservatives could be forgiven for desperately looking around to find a silver lining among all those darkening economic clouds.

And for a short while, it seemed like the president might show a bit of discipline in the area of entitlement reform.

In February 2009, President Obama suggested that Social Security and Medicare should be taken up at the uproariously titled "Fiscal Responsibility Summit." This was the White House get-together that was sponsored by the same liberals who brought you the pork-laden stimulus bill.

Unfortunately for the president and conservatives, House Speaker Nancy Pelosi told Barack Obama she would not allow entitlement reform to be debated in her House.

And why should she?

After all, Democratic consultants have gotten rich through the years by coming up with new and creative ways to scare older voters into believing that any entitlement reform is nothing more than a government conspiracy to throw old people out into the streets.

That's why GOP consultants warned conservative candidates like myself not to reform Social Security or Medicare. The political class called those programs the third rail of American politics, because if you touched them, you were sure to die.

That old rule may have saved scared politicians in the past, but in the Age of Obama, left-wing fear tactics and liberal demagoguery are no match for basic math.

The numbers just don't add up anymore.

George W. Bush realized this in 2005, when he told Americans that he did not want to pass the entitlement crisis on to future presidents.

But Mr. Bush's efforts to save the seniors' entitlement systems were undercut by dishonest Democrats and cowardly Republicans. He was forced to give up on Social Security reform within a year.

With Democrats' well-documented record of shamelessness on the subject, President Obama's announced intention to dig the U.S. entitlement system out of debt was a welcome development.

That was until Nancy Pelosi ordered Mr. Obama to back down.

As was the case with his first stimulus outline, President Obama caved to Ms. Pelosi's pressure and meekly followed the San Francisco speaker's orders.

Instead of addressing the most daunting financial crisis that the United States will face over the next generation, President Obama and his fellow Democrats chose once again to play political games with the programs that provide elderly Americans with medical and financial security.

As the president himself said before being chastened by Ms. Pelosi, "What we have done is kicked this can down the road. We are now at the end of the road and are not in a position to kick it any further. We have to signal seriousness in this by making sure some of the hard decisions are made under my watch, not someone else's."

But kicking the can further down the road is exactly what Democrats did.

It seems ironic that the same liberals who so shamelessly scare senior citizens into believing they are the last great protectors of Social Security are actually the very ones whose inaction threatens that program.

How sad it is that this kind of dishonesty and bad faith would still be rewarded in Washington, D.C.

It is enough to discourage even the most optimistic of people.

Irish playwright Oscar Wilde said that the basis of optimism is sheer terror. He may have had a point. Why else would I cling to my conviction that in spite of Washington politicians, America's greatest chapter has yet to be written?

Terror, I suppose. Absolute terror. Still, I just can't help myself. And if there is a reason for optimism in our current situation, it may be this: the financial crisis of the past year is a wake-up call for all Americans.

The alarm bells that announced the collapse of Bear Stearns and Lehman Brothers, the problems plaguing Fannie Mae and Freddie Mac, the scandals of Bernie Madoff and John Thain may have awakened Americans who have been sleepwalking through history for too long. Once awakened, America's leaders may finally learn that the most basic laws of capitalism (and arithmetic) cannot be altered.

Maybe, just maybe, we have arrived at a teachable moment.

If the financial crisis and the recession it caused tell us anything, it's that there is a great cost to living beyond our means. America's years of living dangerously have caused the first round of economic bombs to detonate.

Perhaps Democrats on Capitol Hill will respond to Mr. Obama's warnings on entitlements before the second round of explosions go off.

Eight years of Republican leadership led to the vaporization of trillions of dollars on entitlement programs, domestic spending, and two major wars. That spending did little to ensure long-term economic growth. Now Democrats have taken control of the nation's checkbook and seem intent on burning through trillions more at a rate that will make Mr. Bush look like a penny-pinching miser.

A TOXIC COCKTAIL OF DEBT

America faces a deadly mix of rising debt, shattered markets, and a deepening recession. And it is our own fault.

There were many, including myself and the editorial page of the *Wall Street Journal,* who warned that this crisis would come sooner or later if Republicans didn't change their ways. Because they didn't, we have even bigger spenders running the White House and Capitol Hill.

But the days of denial are over.

With America's economy on life support, now is the time to take a long look at where we are, where we are going, and what we must do to secure a future that will prove my prescience about America's bright future.

Let's begin our road to recovery by facing some unhappy facts.

As badly as things have been over the past year, the crisis we face today is manageable compared with the long-term collapse our economy will suffer if it refuses to defuse the ticking time bombs that are Washington's gigantic entitlement programs.

America's biggest financial crisis has little to do with bridges to nowhere or yearly deficits. Instead, it is the one-two-three punch of Social Security, Medicare, and Medicaid that most directly threaten the economic survival of the United States over the next generation.

Social Security payroll taxes will soon be unable to fund the benefits promised to millions of senior citizens. Medicare and Medicaid are both on the precipice of collapse.

If health care costs continue to rise, those programs will collapse. The human wreckage will be experienced by every state, every community, every family, every home.

Social Security payroll taxes will explode at the same time benefits to senior citizens and the poor will be cut. Middle-class Americans and the richest among us will all share in the pain, as their parents and grandparents are denied lifesaving treatments.

Hospitals will see their share of health care payments cut in half by Washington and be forced to shut down badly needed services.

Emergency rooms will become even more jammed with those who can't afford treatment. The shortage of qualified doctors and nurses will continue to grow, as fewer bright students decide to work in a health care system on the verge of collapse.

Had such a crisis hit at another time in our country's history, we could spend hundreds of billions of dollars to revive the system. While the deficit spending would have had short-term negative impact, it would have been possible to ease the pressure experienced by these programs.

But with the trillion-dollar bailout of Wall Street, followed by another trillion dollars blown on a sham "stimulus" bill, followed by trillions targeted for bank and real estate bailouts, followed by an almost $4 trillion budget, Washington politicians have drained the well.

We no longer have the money required to sustain the most important parts of our social safety net.

The disastrous state of Social Security is not the only threat to millions of retired Americans. Health insurance coverage for America's seniors (Medicare) and the poor and disabled (Medicaid) also creates daunting challenges and problems that go well beyond those two programs.

Taken together, these three entitlement programs are eating like acid into the solvency of the federal budget.

The budget math is simple: there is an estimated $80 trillion in future entitlement liabilities that are not funded by taxes.

$80,000,000,000,000.00!

As the *Wall Street Journal* wrote in discussing the figure of $1 trillion, "The human mind is not well equipped to fathom a number that large. . . . Homo sapiens hadn't fully evolved a trillion seconds ago: 31,546 years in the past, Neanderthals were still trying to make fire."

After the Democrats' stimulus bill passed into law in February, ads began to run explaining to Americans that if someone had made a million dollars every day from the time Jesus was born until today, they would still not make a trillion dollars.

Now consider that when it comes to entitlements, we're talking about a figure 80 times as large.

Eighty trillion dollars is an amount that is 6 times larger than the *entire* U.S. economy and 16 times larger than the federal debt held by the public. That means even if we did the impossible and paid off our national debt, we would then be required to complete that task 16 more times.

That is, of course, also impossible.

In the end, either Washington politicians will face down the entitlement crisis or America's economic order will collapse. After all, America has been running a Ponzi scheme with entitlement programs that makes Bernie Madoff's crimes look like child's play.

Politicians may want to pretend that they can prop up the entitlement state as it exists today, but no serious economist or politician believes that is possible.

So why won't Nancy Pelosi and Democrats in Congress do

anything to save these programs that are critical to a stable society in the twenty-first century? Because too many politicians prefer pushing off inconvenient truths to giving voters bad news.

TRUTH OR CONSEQUENCES

But my own personal experience taught me that if a politician dared to tell the truth about entitlement programs, voters would respond positively.

Soon after I was elected in the 1994 Republican landslide, President Bill Clinton began accusing Republicans of wanting to cut Medicare to fund tax cuts for the rich.

The attack was low-rent demagoguery, considering that Mr. Clinton had proposed similar cuts the year before. At the same time, Medicare Trust Fund board members were predicting that without our changes, Medicare would go bankrupt.

Unions ran Republican-bashing ads from Florida to California suggesting that we wanted to kick senior citizens out of hospitals to pay off our rich friends at the country club.

As crude as the ad campaign was, it was the Democrats' preferred tactic in the 1996 campaign. I was outraged and spent much of 1996 waiting for the opportunity to rail against any Democrat who dared to use the false attack against me.

That moment came in a debate against my Democratic opponent in the 1996 election. We had been invited to speak at a seniors' group at a local hospital on a variety of issues. The first question was on Medicare.

My opponent followed the Democrats' talking points as he pointed his finger at me and told the seniors, "Joe Scarborough wants to cut your Medicare benefits to fund tax cuts for the rich."

As he finished his answer, I went on the offense, explaining our plan to save Medicare and how my opponent was using fear to win votes. While I won't bore you with the details of that policy debate a decade later, I will tell you that at the end of my first answer, I announced that I would not be talking about any other topic during this debate. I would instead explain to seniors why the tough choices we were making regarding Medicare reform was the only responsible way to save their benefits.

Over the next hour, questions were asked on taxes, education, military spending, and a variety of other topics. But I kept pounding away on why we had to fix the Medicare crisis.

At the end of the debate, my opponent left the room mumbling incoherently. He never brought up the subject again.

Social Security and Medicare are wildly popular with the segment that turns out to vote in the highest number: senior citizens. More than any other demographic group, they can be counted on to swing elections. Seniors can also be relied on to treat any efforts to change Social Security and Medicare with responses ranging from great skepticism to fierce opposition. That's why bluntly addressing the issue may just be the safest political approach.

After all, the greatest challenge to U.S. entitlement programs comes down once again to basic math.

Since demographics is destiny when it comes to entitlement programs, we need to admit that some disturbing trends will soon add up to big trouble.

When Social Security was launched in the 1930s, life expectancy was about the same number as the age an American could start drawing from the system.

It was a Ponzi scheme that worked pretty well.

In 1940, there were 160 workers paying into the Social Security system for every one that was drawing a benefit.

In 1950, there were 16 workers for every one on Social Security.

Today, there are three workers paying into the system for every one that is drawing from that system. Soon, that employee number will move closer to two.

Over the last generation, baby boomers financed the U.S. entitlement system and kept benefits flowing to an aging population. But with those same boomers retiring in the twenty-first century, the numbers will soon stop adding up.

Sadly, many Republicans won't admit to that truth. Democrats seem to be even more reluctant.

But if current politicians are too cowardly to reform the programs, future politicians will have few good choices.

They could fight to protect the status quo in these systems, but that would crowd out tax dollars for all other priorities, including national defense. Future leaders' only other option would be to raise taxes to rates that rival Soviet-style confiscation.

If nothing is done to reform the system, workers over the next generation will be shackled with federal tax rates that will suck anywhere from 55 percent to 80 percent of their salaries.

The U.S. entitlement programs are a legacy of the New Deal of the 1930s and the Great Society of the 1960s. They were designed for another era but haven't been modernized to keep up with the times.

Long ago they became unsustainable.

Today they endanger the future of America.

It's time for conservatives of all parties to start telling voters the truth. Reform is long overdue—so let's get started.

THE KING OF ALL PONZIS

The first step in understanding the Social Security crisis is to understand that the payroll tax does not provide enough revenue to fund both programs.

The tax dollars you think you're paying in order to guarantee "social security" are not doing anything of the sort. All they are doing is allowing the political class to promise that you'll receive government checks when you retire.

In reality, the money you are "investing" for your Social Security is being spent by politicians today on thousands of federal programs that have *nothing* to do with Social Security.

But how could this be?

Didn't Democrats fight George W. Bush's Social Security plan by telling us endlessly in 2004 that Social Security didn't need to be reformed because the program was actually running a surplus?

They did. And the truth is that Social Security is currently taking in more money than it is paying out. But what your friends on the left won't tell you is that Social Security is a pay-as-you-go program. That means that your Social Security taxes go straight into Congress's general fund, so they have more money to spend on whatever pet projects they wish to fund.

Here's why.

Politicians in Washington have always played a shell game with entitlement money. They tell us that there is something called a Social Security Trust Fund, but no such creature actually exists.

Instead, the surplus dollars are transferred to the government's general budget and used to pay for all the other spending that gets shoveled in and out of Congress's door every year.

What this means is that when payroll taxes are taken out of your paycheck, they do not go to pay for your retirement. Instead, part of them pays for a beneficiary from a previous generation.

None of your money goes toward savings and investment for your retirement. And unlike the lucky retiree whose Social Security account you are filling, you may find that there is no one around to pay your retirement benefits when you are old enough to retire.

Because there used to be so many workers for every retired person getting benefits, the payroll tax Americans had to pay into the system was small compared with the benefits received by retirees—only about 2 percent on the first $3,000 of income. The first several generations of Americans who left the workforce under Social Security earned fantastic returns.

Those who retired in 1940 enjoyed a 114 percent return.

But the system began to show strain as the size of benefits increased about the same time the number of workers paying into the system fell.

Starting in the 1950s and continuing through the late 1970s, politicians seemed to compete to see who could promise the most benefits to the largest group of retirees.

Since seniors have always been reliable voters, those promises were good politics.

But they added up to bad economics.

The demographics that allowed pay-as-you-go Social Security to work so well in past generations have continued to sour ever since. Birthrates have fallen drastically while life expectancy has continued to soar. And the number of contributors to the system will continue to fall while the number of retirees using the system will rise exponentially.

Because the ratio of workers to retirees continues to fall, payroll taxes continue to rise—and now stand at 12.4 percent of your salary.

Real rates of return are also plunging. A worker who retires in 2025 will earn less than 2 percent on his Social Security taxes over his lifetime. Remember, that's down from the 114 percent people got if they retired in 1940.

Over the next twenty years, almost all baby boomers will move into their retirement years. That, in turn, will lead to a mass exodus from the workforce.

The number of retirees drawing Social Security will jump from 47 million today to 77 million in the not-so-distant future.

The Social Security system will start running a deficit over the next decade when benefits exceed annual payroll tax revenue.

The Trust Fund "surplus" will not even exist on paper over the next generation. By that time, Social Security will rely solely on cash from payroll taxes paid into the system that year. Because there will be so few workers paying the benefits of so many retirees, either future generations will be crushed by taxes or seniors will be thrown under the bus.

If nothing is done in Washington soon to avert this crisis, chances are good that both workers and seniors will feel unbearable financial pain.

But when it comes to an entitlement cash crunch, the pay-as-you-go scheme is already driving these programs into debt. Today, Social Security and Medicare combined eat up almost 5 percent of federal income tax revenues.

In the next decade, one in seven income tax dollars will be pushed over into Social Security to keep that system afloat.

By 2020, entitlements for the elderly will consume 25 percent of all income tax dollars. By 2030, they will eat up a staggering 50 percent of all income taxes.

To put that in perspective, over the next thirty years Washington politicians will have to slash every government program on the books by 50 percent just to keep paying out benefits for two entitlement programs. By mid-century, when my twenty-one-year-old son retires, 75 percent of all federal income taxes will go to paying his retirement benefits.

In our children's lifetime, the U.S. government will have to use every dime it takes in to keep Social Security and Medicare solvent.

That means there will be no money for national defense, education programs, environmental protections, federal courts, interstate highways, or any other legislative priority. Every dime Washington gets will go to feeding the exploding costs of two runaway entitlement programs.

If we continue with today's underlying fiscal policy—no changes in benefits, no changes in taxes, no additional programs—spending on Social Security, Medicare, and Medicaid will climb from 18 percent of the economy today to 28 percent in 2050 and to 35 percent in seventy-five years.

If tax revenues remain constant over that same period, the federal debt will explode, rising to more than 290 percent of our GDP in 2050.

That is a debt that will crush America.

AMERICA'S DEATH SPIRAL?

If left unchecked, these three programs would drain the nation's pool of savings and make it impossible to invest. As investment dwindled, workers' wages would stagnate and interest rates would rise.

We could try to borrow more from abroad, but only months into the Obama presidency, most countries are already wary of accumulating more debt from the United States. Imagine how much more skeptical foreign investors would become in the midst of a severe entitlement crisis.

Our government would be forced to try anyway to finance its interest payments by issuing more debt, the deficit would explode faster than the economy grew, and tax revenues would dry up.

This likely scenario would lead to a vicious circle in which government would be forced to issue more debt in order to pay ever-higher interest rates. Within fifty years, the sophisticated economic models that allow us to make such projections would crash—the deficits having become so large and unsustainable that those models can't even grasp the economic apocalypse this entitlement crisis would spawn.

It is a nightmare scenario that could result in the bankruptcy of

America, the collapse of U.S. society, and the unleashing of a global depression.

Conservatives dedicated to preserving social order have a duty to take prudent steps to begin the painful process of reforming Social Security, Medicare, and Medicaid. The alternative is not an option for any leader who loves his country.

Saving these programs will be difficult, since there is no realistic tax increase that could sustain the promised levels of benefits for Social Security, Medicare, and Medicaid. If those promises were financed with an across-the-board increase in individual and corporate income tax rates, the rates would have to more than double. According to the nonpartisan Congressional Budget Office,

> The tax rate for the lowest tax bracket would have to be increased from 10 percent to 25 percent; the tax rate on incomes in the current 25 percent bracket would have to be increased to 63 percent; and the tax rate of the highest bracket would have to be raised from 35 percent to 88 percent. The top corporate income tax rate would also increase from 35 percent to 88 percent. Such tax rates would significantly reduce economic activity.

Let me break that down for you.

To maintain these three entitlement programs at current benefit levels, the United States would have to adopt a tax system that is roughly the equivalent of North Korea's.

Such a punitive tax system would lead, of course, to a collapse in living standards and the meltdown of America's economic activity. Because of these confiscatory tax rates, those systems we were trying to save would eventually dry up regardless of our taxing efforts.

When FDR signed the Social Security Act, he said its most important mission was to provide "protection against poverty-ridden old age." But now the entitlement state is clamped down in a bear trap of its own making.

Its popularity with seniors means that politicians of all parties fear doing what it takes to save the program if it means a reduction in benefits or an increase in costs to beneficiaries.

But regardless of what senior citizen advocacy groups say, the day of reckoning for Social Security and Medicare is coming. And the crisis will only become more extreme when all the baby boomers retire.

The fraction of voters receiving benefits relative to those paying taxes will increase by 50 percent in 20 years and double in 50 years—making reform even more difficult.

Few Washington politicians are ready to face up to such stubborn facts. One politician who did challenge the status quo was George W. Bush.

While his privatization scheme was considered risky by many, Mr. Bush did use his reelection to do what no previous president has ever done: he used political capital to try to reform an untouchable entitlement program.

CRISIS? WHAT CRISIS?

In his 2005 state of the union address, President Bush called Social Security a great moral success of the twentieth century, but he also told Americans it was headed toward bankruptcy. He explained that if nothing was done to reform the program, the only solutions would be drastically higher taxes, massive new borrowing, or sudden and severe cuts in Social Security benefits.

President Bush believed that Congress should debate the possibility of limiting benefits for wealthy retirees, indexing benefits to prices rather than wages, increasing the retirement age, discouraging early collection of Social Security benefits, and changing the way benefits are calculated.

He also endorsed the idea of voluntary personal retirement accounts.[1]

According to Mr. Bush,

> All these ideas are on the table. I know that none of these reforms would be easy. But we have to move ahead with courage and honesty, because our children's retirement security is more important than partisan politics. I will work with members of Congress to find the most effective combination of reforms. I will listen to anyone who has a good idea to offer.

Predictably, the Bush plan failed.

National media outlets used the GOP president's much-needed call for reform as a chance to draw political blood. Many of the same newspapers and TV networks that had been claiming that there was a crisis in the system over the past decade suddenly claimed that there was no crisis after all.

It was like a surreal scene out of *The Simpsons* when Chief Wiggum stands in front of a burning UFO and tells the residents of Springfield, "Nothing to see here. Move along."

---

1 The way voluntary personal accounts would work is that younger workers would be able to set aside part of their money in their own retirement account. The money would only go into a conservative mix of bonds and stock funds. There were good options to protect investments from sudden market swings on the eve of retirement, and steps to ensure that a personal account couldn't be emptied out all at once, but rather would have to be paid out over time, as an addition to traditional Social Security benefits. In addition, personal retirement accounts would start gradually, with the yearly limits on contributions being raised in stages, eventually permitting all workers to set aside 4 percentage points of their payroll taxes in their accounts. Personal retirement accounts were patterned after the Thrift Savings Plan, which lets federal workers deposit a portion of their paychecks into any of five different broadly based investment funds.

Democrats were even more irresponsible by refusing to add any constructive ideas. Instead, they were simply interested in using the president's decision to tell the truth about Social Security to bludgeon Bush and Republicans.

Republicans, in turn, lost their nerve. Even though they controlled both chambers of Congress, a Social Security bill never even made its way out of committee.

Throughout the debate, the American public remained ambivalent about the president's effort to save Social Security and strengthen America's long-term economic health.

It was a terrible, head-buried-in-the-sand display all the way around.

History will reflect that in the Bush era, only the president seemed interested in saving Social Security. It was a missed opportunity of epic proportions.

Unfortunately, the crisis is even more extreme with Medicare. That program is growing at a faster rate and has a long-term debt that is six times larger than Social Security's. And eight years of Republicanism just made the situation worse.

Ironically, the same George Bush who showed so much courage on Social Security actually made the looming Medicare crisis even graver by adding a $7 trillion prescription drug benefit to it.

Supporters of the president argue that the $7 trillion Medicare drug plans contain health savings accounts that most conservatives love. They also claim the drug benefit is working better than predicted.

More than 1,800 private plans are competing for enrollment. Medicare beneficiaries like the program, with 85 percent saying they are satisfied with it. And little wonder: in 2008, the average beneficiary premium was just under $25 per month, well below the original estimate of $41.

In addition, the program's competitive design is holding down costs a bit more than originally expected for the U.S. government.

The Centers for Medicare and Medicaid Services announced in 2008 that the new drug benefit's cost will be 40 percent—or $250 billion—less over ten years than was originally projected.

Beyond that, Mr. Bush wanted to reform the rest of the program too. He pushed for "premium support" for future Medicare enrollees as a way to convert the program toward a controlled voucher with competition. He aggressively worked to get this kind of idea started in the program, and Congress balked every time, including Republican speaker Denny Hastert and Senate leader Bill Frist.

Predictably, Democrats never offered a serious reform of Medicare.

The great flaw in President Bush's Medicare plan was that he spent $7 trillion in entitlement spending that the Medicare program did not have. As David Stockman chronicled in *The Triumph of Politics,* Ronald Reagan committed a similar fiscal sin, passing popular tax cuts before attempting to counterbalance that tax relief with spending cuts.

Like Mr. Bush's comprehensive Medicare reform plans, Ronald Reagan's spending cuts never became law. The net result for both failures was a more oppressive public debt.

Baby boomer demographics will place the same disastrous pressures on Medicare that now burden Social Security. But demographics only tells part of the story.

Equally damaging for the long-term solvency of Medicare will be the continued growth of health care costs.

HIGH COSTS HAZARDOUS TO YOUR HEALTH

In 2008, Americans spent $2.4 trillion—16.6 percent of the economy—to meet their health needs.

By 2012, health spending is projected to exceed $3 trillion, or 17.7 percent of GDP.

Even with those massive outlays, almost 47 million people are still uninsured. And despite the fact that Washington has wasted years throwing money at the health care problem instead of containing costs, President Obama has proposed another $634 billion "down payment" on socializing Medicine. This despite the fact that any serious health care expert will tell you the greatest challenge facing the health care system is exploding costs.

If the growth of per capita health care spending exceeds the rate of growth of per capita GDP by merely 2 percentage points—and that's optimistic—then health care spending will consume almost 80 percent of GDP by 2075.

Under those assumptions, Medicare and Medicaid will grow by nearly four times as a share of the economy by 2050. They will also take up as much GDP as *the entire federal budget* does today, which includes Medicare and Medicaid.

In 2008, the Medicare Trustees reported that 2007 expenditures for Medicare were $432 billion, or 3.2 percent of GDP. Over the next generation, these expenditures will explode. The combination of rising health care costs and aging baby boomers will be too much for the current system to endure.

This means that in the first half of this century, Medicare will consume about one of every ten dollars made in America. If you throw in Medicaid, almost 20 percent of America's total economy will be devoured by these programs. To put that in perspective, that is a higher percentage of GDP than the entire federal government consumed my last year in Congress.

As with Social Security, time is not on our side.

The Medicare Trustees warned, "The longer action is delayed, the greater the required adjustments will be, the larger the burden on future generations, and the more severe the detrimental economic impact on our nation."

Medicare's total unfunded liability is *$70.8 trillion*. That's about $20 trillion more than the value of the entire world economy in

2007. Even if every business and worker that exists on the face of the earth today devoted everything they earned over one year to make just one of America's entitlement programs solvent, it *still* wouldn't cover the bill.

Ring up the handbasket, because we are going straight to hell.

Conservatives can get America out of this mess by beginning to act conservative again. That means putting tired dogma behind us and pulling out the calculator.

While conservatives from Barry Goldwater to Ronald Reagan have championed privatization of these programs, the political reality is that as enlightened as that approach may be, such legislation will never pass.

Never.

Get over it.

I understand that if the 1983 Social Security Reform Commission had actually implemented voluntary accounts, the estimate is that over $7 trillion of additional wealth would have been created because of them. And the Social Security system would now be on a much sounder foundation.

I also know that under Republican privatization plans, if the total benefit for someone with a personal account fell below currently promised Social Security benefits, the federal government would send that person a check each month to make up the difference.

Since Republican reformers tell us that only a few workers would fall below the guarantee, and as the taxpayers would only be making up the difference, the burden of the guarantee would be dramatically smaller than the burden of the current system.

But privatization plans for these programs will not pass anytime in the next decade, and the conservative movement cannot continue to throw itself on the barricade of privatization as the entitlement time bomb ticks down to zero.

With America's economic solvency at stake, now is the time for we conservatives to behave conservatively and face the facts as they are, not as we wish they would be.

We don't have time to wait for ideological perfection.

THE ONLY CONSERVATIVE SOLUTION

So what do we do with Social Security, Medicare, and Medicaid?

While they seem destined for life support, we all know that they have become an integral part of American society. Politicians will never get rid of these systems, nor should conservatives want them eliminated.

Since we traditionally support institutions that bring stability to a society, it is important for us all to face the fact that Social Security and Medicare have become a part of the twenty-first century's American social contract.

Medicare assures our society's senior citizens health care at an affordable cost. That guarantee could cripple our country if its growth remains unchecked. So we must do what is necessary to make decisions that will stabilize our economy while guaranteeing health care to our parents and grandparents—even if it is ideologically challenging to some core beliefs about the state's rightful role.

Seniors are facing ever-higher costs out of pocket, and budget-driven policies are causing doctors and hospitals across the country to close their practices to Medicare patients.

Social Security will also have its legs cut out from under it inside of a decade. After that, it will collapse in the blink of an eye, causing the greatest pain to seniors.

So what can conservatives do?

We should start by urging Barack Obama to keep the pressure on Nancy Pelosi and Harry Reid. Despite President Obama's brash partisan approach in his first months in office, he should try to reclaim the bipartisan banner by forcing leaders from all parties to sit in a room and hammer out a compromise plan that would leave everyone unhappy but would save Social Security and Medicare.

Since Democrats rule Washington at present, it would actually provide the president cover if he did bring Republican leaders into the talks. Without them, Democrats would follow Nancy Pelosi's lead and continue "kicking the can down the road."

It has been said that only a conservative like Nixon could go to China. By the same logic, perhaps only a liberal like Barack Obama could reform Social Security and Medicare.

In 1983, the commission method bought Social Security a few more decades when it faced an immediate cash crunch because of a recession and high inflation. No politician wanted to be the one forced to make hard decisions, yet they had no choice. There was political pain, but with that came policy gains. Social Security was saved temporarily.

In 2009, we find ourselves on the edge of another financial cliff. The question now is whether Barack Obama will follow Ronald Reagan's example and force Congress to get serious over entitlement reform.

Every option will be put on the table, and every conservative must realize that the most irresponsible thing they can do is nothing.

A conservative conserves. Regardless of the pain involved. And make no mistake about it: saving Social Security, Medicare, and Medicaid will cause great political pain for all sides.

Just look at the grim political options that will be undertaken to save these systems over the next generation:

- raising taxes

- making seniors pay for more of their benefits

- cutting benefits for higher-income seniors

- raising the age at which seniors become eligible for benefits

Every proposal listed would be political suicide under normal circumstances, but these are not ordinary times. Conservatives must promote economic stability and social order now and in the future.

One way to do that is by telling all Americans 55 years of age and older that their benefits will be unaffected. That will prevent seniors' organizations and demagogic politicians from scaring older Americans to win votes.

We could tell those who are 50 to 54 that their benefits would be altered on the margins.

But future generations have to know that the only way they will ever get Social Security or Medicare will be through dramatic reforms.

As I wrote earlier, life expectancy used to be about the same as when Social Security benefits began. But today, life expectancy is approaching eighty. Therefore it makes sense that Americans in their twenties, thirties, and forties know that they will receive their first Social Security check when they turn 70 years of age.

Young Americans should expect that number to rise as Americans live healthier, longer lives.

And let's face it. Any plan that saves Social Security, Medicare, and Medicaid will have to raise taxes, cut benefits, and conserve health care for Americans who are under 55.

Any politician who tells you our system can be saved under existing political realities is a liar.

If our leaders in Washington get serious with entitlement reform, expect compromises to be made that will be offensive ideologically to the conservative movement. Also expect liberals to flinch at the sacrifices their side will have to endure, as politicians on the left will face grief for "shredding the safety net."

Unfortunately for all sides, America finds itself at a stage in this entitlement crisis where everyone is going to have to give until it hurts.

And in the words of singer Sarah McLaughlin, "This is going to hurt like hell."

But any painful compromise will be better than the alternative, which is the collapse of Social Security, Medicare, Medicaid, and the U.S. economy.

We have no choice but to make our entitlement system solvent. It is the only way to guarantee that America has a fighting chance to restore its long-term economic stability. But that will only happen if we all start working now to defuse this ticking time bomb.

There is no time to waste.

8 WHAT REPUBLICANISM HATH WROUGHT

HOW CHOOSING POWER OVER PRINCIPLE COST CONSERVATIVES BOTH

> Those who have been once intoxicated with power, and have derived any kind of emolument from it, even though but for one year, never can willingly abandon it. They may be distressed in the midst of all their power; but they will never look to anything but power for their relief.
>
> —*Edmund Burke*

> We Republicans came to power in 1994 to change government, and government changed us. And that's why we lost the election: We began to value power over principle.
>
> —*John McCain*

What a long, strange trip it's been.

A decade ago this month, I flew to Austin, Texas, with a group of Florida leaders to meet the man we believed would be the next president of the United States.

Few of us stopped long enough to ask why Governor George W. Bush had been christened the conservative movement's answer to eight years of Clintonism. But 18 months before election night, an aura of inevitability had already begun to settle around the 41st president's son.

After walking into the Texas governor's mansion, I was met immediately by George Bush.

He was shorter, thinner, and more Southern in affect than his brother, who was Florida's governor. And while Jeb won over converts with his intelligence, his brother George was more comfortable around people and connected immediately with everyone who walked through the door.

During that meeting a decade ago, it took Governor Bush only a few minutes to win over the most skeptical conservatives in the room. The Texan promised that his administration would unite America, balance the budget, keep Washington bureaucrats out of local classrooms, and run a humble foreign policy.

For a congressman who had spent the past five years fighting Bill Clinton to reduce spending, abolish the federal education bureaucracy, and limit military adventurism, the governor's words were a welcome relief.

But remembering those promises 10 years later, it is hard to imagine how any politician could have strayed further from his stated policy plans than did Mr. Bush.

Soon after arriving in Washington, the 43rd president teamed up with Teddy Kennedy to pass the biggest expansion of the education bureaucracy in U.S. history. "No Child Left Behind" made Republicans reverse their positions on education reform overnight.

Just five years earlier, more than 150 conservatives in Congress had signed on to my bill to eliminate Washington's education bureaucracy and return that money, power, and authority back to local classrooms. "The Back to Basics" education reform package was even adopted in the 1996 House Budget Resolution.

But five years later, many of these same Republicans joined Senator Kennedy and George Bush in passing a bill that left no education bureaucrat behind. Their president's 180-degree change made small-government conservatives look like hypocrites.

But that was only the beginning.

Republicans' record on spending also took a radical turn for the worse.

Throughout the Clinton years, the GOP Congress had fought Bill Clinton to balance the budget and pay down the national debt. By the time George Bush stepped into the White House, conservatives including Steve Largent, Mark Sanford, and I had passed along a hard-fought $155 billion surplus to the new Republican administration.

We believed that budget surpluses would be the rule in a newly restrained Congress. But that massive surplus would disappear and Republicans would create a $500 billion deficit within a few short years. By the time Mr. Bush left Washington, the deficit would surpass $1 trillion.

As with their flip-flop on education, these transformed Republicans would once again choose party loyalty over conservative principles.

Budget battles with big-spending presidents were now a thing of the past for the GOP. This president would get whatever he wanted from Congress, even if it bankrupted America. After all, he *was* a Republican.

For the next eight years, Republicanism was a slavish devotion to consolidating political power instead of advancing conservative values.

Republicanism was the justification of all means to reach the ends of a monopoly on power and a permanent GOP majority. But, instead of conquering, Republicanism crippled a conservative movement built over 50 years by William Buckley and Ronald Reagan.

Republicanism also got the better of conservatives in the areas of war and peace.

The same president who promised in the 2000 presidential campaign to conduct a "humble" foreign policy saw his international outlook radically altered by the events of September 11.

That made sense. But what did not was the loss of all ideological bearings by conservatives when it came to how their leaders should conduct foreign policy.

"WOODROW WILSON LIVES!"

During the Age of Clinton, Republicans had been champions of Casper Weinberger's and Colin Powell's conservative doctrine on war.

The Weinberger-Powell Doctrine urged restraint when using military force. The former secretary of defense and secretary of state supported troop deployment only if all other options had been exhausted.

General Powell, whose outlook had been shaped by the tragedy of Vietnam, also argued that U.S. troops should never be sent to a war zone unless Washington politicians gave them all the military might they needed to win.

Powell believed that once the terrible decision was made to go to war, the United States should not seek a fair fight. Instead, it should use decisive force to crush its enemy as quickly as possible. Then U.S. troops should return home.

But the same Republicans who had quoted Powell's doctrine repeatedly throughout the 1990s tossed it aside in the name of party unity as their president pressed for war. Had GOP leaders been more loyal to their conservative convictions than their party bosses, Secretary of Defense Donald Rumsfeld would have been forced to give generals the troops they needed for victory instead of trying to win the Iraq War on the cheap.

Had conservatives remained consistent in their calls for decisive force for *all* military wars, Iraq would not have devolved into chaos. But again, Republicanism applied a different standard to presidents based on their party affiliation.

Because party loyalty again proved to be a more powerful pull than past principles, U.S. troops were forced to repeat the mistakes of Vietnam that the Weinberger-Powell doctrines were specifically created to prevent.

Conservative commitment to first principles was equally absent when it came to entitlement spending.

Most GOP members went quietly along with the Bush White House when it decided to take a crippled Medicare program and add an additional $7,000,000,000.00 liability by passing the Medicare drug benefit plan.

How any self-described conservative president could sign the largest expansion of an entitlement program in U.S. history is confounding enough. But when you consider the program was already racing toward bankruptcy, the president's $7 trillion plan seems all the more inexplicable.

The Medicare debacle may have been the best example of how Republicanism allowed the pursuit of power to rot the conservative movement to its core.

Few GOP leaders in Congress or the media dared to stand up to their own president. Too many justified their blind faith by convincing themselves and others that telling the truth about Republican leaders would help the Democratic Party.

Ironically, it was their enabling silence that led to the party's total collapse. Remaining quiet about the president's failures in Iraq, on the budget, with entitlement spending, and during Hurricane Katrina prevented the Bush White House from taking a corrective course until the Republican Party's destruction was inevitable.

Conservatives have always believed that ideas have consequences.

After the Bush era, they learned just how high the cost was for betraying their beliefs.

Barack Obama's transformation of Washington was made possible by the GOP's failures. Put another way, the return of the old welfare state through Mr. Obama would never have happened had our leaders chosen conservatism over Republicanism.

WE HAVE MET THE ENEMY AND IT IS US

Politically, it is hard to imagine how any Democratic politician could have damaged the Republican brand more than its own leaders.

When I was elected to Congress in 1994, Republicans held two congressional seats in Maine, two in New Hampshire, two in Massachusetts, and three in Connecticut.

Six years later, when Mr. Bush was sworn into office for the first time, Republicans still controlled House and Senate seats in Maine, New Hampshire, Vermont, Rhode Island, Massachusetts, and Connecticut.

Today, the Republican Party does not represent a single New England voter in the U.S. House of Representatives.

The GOP's fortunes nationwide are similarly grim.

Republicans' failures have allowed Democrats to begin dominating other regions of America as well. Long gone are the days when Republican candidates like Richard Nixon and Ronald Reagan could post historic landslides with 49 of 50 states going "red."

As columnist Ron Brownstein noted after the 2008 election, Democrats now have a lock on almost 250 of the 270 electoral votes needed every four years to win the White House.

In the five presidential elections from 1992 forward, Republicans have lost the same 18 states and the District of Columbia every time. That means the Democrats have been able to start every election cycle needing to find no more than 22 electoral votes to win the presidency.

It gets worse.

The Republican Party is so weak in those 18 states and the District of Columbia that John McCain lost all of those contests by more than 10 points. The Republican nominee lost Washington, D.C., by 84 percentage points. Worse yet for GOP fortunes, Democrats control 33 of the 36 Senate seats from those solidly blue states.

That is a dramatic reversal for a party who believed they were building a permanent majority just five years ago.

Following Mr. Bush's victory over Senator John Kerry in 2004, Republicans held 231 seats in the House and 55 in the Senate.

Many Washington insiders began citing the Republicans' 31-seat majority over the Democrats in the House and the 11-seat Senate majority as evidence of an everlasting GOP hegemony. Karl Rove was declared the political genius of our time, and the Republican machine was on a perpetual roll.

I was skeptical.

In the same year others were predicting a permanent GOP majority, I wrote *Rome Wasn't Burnt in a Day.* It was a critical look at Mr. Bush's spending record and a warning of dark days to come for my former colleagues.

In *Rome* I predicted the Republican Party's collapse and told of a growing danger to the U.S. economy if conservatives refused to get America's financial house in order. To avoid a political and economic disaster, I wrote that Republicans would have to put conservative values over party loyalties once again.

They didn't.

The reaction to my criticisms was fierce, as it was two years later when I wrote a *Washington Post* opinion piece warning Republican candidates to distance themselves from President Bush and Donald Rumsfeld's disastrous approach in Iraq.

I suggested that candidates should spend the next 50 days of the 2006 campaign telling conservatives and liberals the following: "President Bush and Defense Secretary Donald H. Rumsfeld were wrong to think that the nation could win Iraq on the cheap."

I then told Republican candidates that if they wanted to remain in the majority, they would also have to admit to voters that the White House had been reckless with taxpayer dollars.

"I would also look them in the eye and say that our president was wrong to believe that the United States could fight two wars, cut taxes, and increase federal spending, all at once," I wrote.

Once again, Republican candidates chose Republicanism over conservatism. They chose instead to remain silent. The result was a political and economic disaster we will be paying for over the next generation.

REPUBLICANISM CRUSHES CONSERVATISM

GOP members decided it was more important to continue worshipping at the feet of Republicanism than it was to lead like conservatives. The result of their sycophancy again backfired as those politicians who feared telling the truth about their party because it might cost them power ended up losing their seats in Congress. They also cost us the Republican majority.

Republicans in 2006 would have done well to remember the scripture verse that says "He that fears for his life will lose it."

Maybe I am being presumptuous, but I would guess that the same White House that treated dissent as politically treasonous could have benefited from a few more honest brokers around the West Wing. Had they not feared free and open debates within the White House, perhaps Iraq, Katrina, and the Wall Street crisis would have turned out differently.

Spineless Republicans who avoided speaking up out of fear did the president of the United States no more of a favor than did

Elvis's entourage when they enabled the King of Rock and Roll to feed his gluttony. You can feed a king's appetites for only so long before his own excesses destroy him.

For President Bush, the refusal to listen to a myriad of dissenting opinions and absorb bad news was his ultimate political undoing.

Think about it.

How would the Iraq War have been different if a few senior Republican senators had decided to fight back when Donald Rumsfeld bullied members of Congress over troop levels in Iraq?

What if one senior Armed Services member had told Mr. Rumsfeld that his "light footprint" strategy was a betrayal of every lesson learned by conservatives after Vietnam?

And what if more congressmen had put conservatism above Republicanism in the early Bush years?

Our deficit would now be smaller, our national debt would now be manageable, and our financial house would be better prepared to meet the challenges ahead.

We would also likely be confronting these challenges with a Republican Congress and president.

If only more conservatives had put principle above power, the political world would be a much different place today.

How do I know?

Because I quickly learned in Congress that Andrew Jackson was right: one man with courage makes a majority. I saw conservatives like Oklahoma senator Tom Coburn and Arizona congressman Matt Salmon stand up for conservative principles over political loyalties. Leading with courage and convictions paid off.

Along the way I learned that one man may be a majority, but ten who fear nothing can change America.

In 1994, the Republican Party was swept into power with the help of 74 GOP freshmen. As a group we were younger, more conservative, and less experienced than most politicians who make it to Congress. But our ignorance of the system ended up being our greatest strength.

We spent our first months in Washington being lectured on the finer points of how Capitol Hill really worked. More to the point, we were being told that freshman congressmen were expected to sit down and shut up.

Freshman members do not usually confront appropriations chairmen, especially when they are of the same party.

We did.

Freshman members are not supposed to offer amendments to kill a senior member's pet project at home.

We did.

Freshman members cannot criticize their own leaders in national newspapers for being insufficiently conservative.

But we did.

And freshman members do not publicly challenge the most powerful speaker of the house in decades and tell him to start acting like a conservative or get out of town.

We did.

I cannot remember all the times I found myself locked in small rooms with conservatives like Mark Sanford, Steve Largent, and Tom Coburn strategizing over how to keep the pressure on Speaker Newt Gingrich and Bill Clinton to cut taxes and balance the budget.

We knew that challenging our own speaker could cause the premature end to our political careers, but none of us cared. We had come to Washington as Americans first, conservatives second, and Republicans last.

It sounds melodramatic now, but we really were willing to lose everything politically to change the way Washington worked.

And for a while, we did.

Republican leaders and most of the old bulls in the Republican caucus were less than inspired by our zeal.

That a handful of freshman congressmen could challenge the most powerful speaker since Sam Rayburn struck many Capitol Hill veterans as preposterous. But in the end, it wasn't.

We pushed Gingrich to stand firm on those conservative principles that helped create our majority in 1994. And because we stood on principle, our small group of rebels soon gained support from conservative groups nationwide.

By 1998, Gingrich was out as speaker.

The same old bulls that had attacked us for going after their beloved speaker were now patting us on the back, thanking us for getting him out of their way.

Newt Gingrich was a visionary conservative who accomplished great things as speaker. But like many who gain power in Washington, he forgot why he was elected speaker. He has since regained his conservative footing and is again an indispensible intellectual voice on the right. But in 1999, very few conservatives missed him after he left Congress.

THIS TOWN'S NOT BIG ENOUGH FOR THE BOTH OF US

Following my 2006 *Washington Post* op-ed, I again found myself surrounded by Republican critics in the media, in Congress, and at the White House.

A governor who was up for reelection asked me to speak at an event in his home state soon after that editorial was published. When the White House found out that I would be involved, they called the governor and told him President Bush would not show up if I attended.

The embarrassed governor called me at home to apologize, saying the White House had told him his state "was not big enough for President Bush and Joe Scarborough."

But as I predicted in the *Washington Post,* the Republican Party was routed in the 2006 congressional elections. The GOP went from enjoying a majority of 30 seats in the House to being in the minority by that same number.

The 60-seat swing was a stunning turnaround for Mr. Bush and his "permanent majority."

Republicans also lost control of the Senate.

A day after his party suffered its worst collapse in a generation, Bush finally fired Rumsfeld. It struck me as interesting that the same president who had been angered by my criticism of Rumsfeld before the election sacked him the day after.

The Republican president also belatedly began talking about runaway spending in Congress, as I had in my preelection critiques of my party. Unfortunately, these deathbed conversions came too late to save the Republican majority.

The Republican Party's collapse continued through the 2008 elections, with Barack Obama enjoying the greatest victory margin since Lyndon Johnson's rout of Barry Goldwater in 1964.

Republicans also suffered another round of staggering losses in the Senate, with Democrats capturing 59 seats.

In the House they enjoyed almost unprecedented success, with back-to-back electoral landslides in 2006 and 2008.

Americans who had trusted the Grand Old Party to protect their tax dollars, support the troops, and shrink the federal bureaucracy let Republican candidates know of their anger at the polls. The GOP was swept completely from power, and for good reason.

Eight years of Republicanism led to

- the worst U.S. financial crisis in 75 years and the worst recession of the last 25

- the largest annual deficit in U.S. history

- the largest national debt in U.S. history

- the largest trade deficit in U.S. history

- the largest expansion of government spending since LBJ's Great Society

- the largest expansion of the federal education bureaucracy in U.S. history

- the collapse of the Republican majority in the U.S. House

- the collapse of the Republican majority in the U.S. Senate

- the loss of the White House to Barack Obama, a man rated as the Senate's most liberal member

- the nationalization of America's banking sector

- the political and intellectual crack-up of the Republican Party

- the destruction of Ronald Reagan's conservative coalition

After eight years of Republicanism, can anyone guarantee voters that Republicans will be conservative with Americans' tax dollars if they are ever put back in control?

After eight years of Republicanism, can conservatives promise Americans that their best hope for balanced budgets, lower taxes, and greater freedom rests with the Republican Party?

And after eight years of Republicanism, can conservative leaders ever guarantee Americans that if put back in charge of the federal government, they will change Washington instead of allowing Washington to change them?

Those are the questions conservatives must answer for themselves before they begin the process of rebuilding the shattered remnants of the party left after eight years of Republicanism.

Fifty years ago, William F. Buckley wrote *Up from Liberalism* to propose a series of conservative alternatives to the dominant political ideology of his day.

In that classic work, Mr. Buckley vowed to resist the centralized state's continued march toward greater control over individuals' lives.

A half-century later, we would all do well to refocus on Mr. Buckley's vision for a conservative movement. With federal spending reaching death-defying heights, with Barack Obama's rebuilding of the old welfare state, and with the federal debt reaching crippling new levels under Democratic domination, America must once again move up from liberalism.

But first we need to *move up from Republicanism.*

Winston Churchill once famously said of democracy that it was the worst form of government except for all others that had been tried.

I suppose it may provide cold comfort for GOP partisans to argue the same about their party. But the Republican Party will not regain power by simply attacking Democrats.

Ronald Reagan did not define himself by Jimmy Carter's weakness. Reagan was exceptional because of his own gifts, just as Margaret Thatcher and Pope John Paul II were historical figures because of their individual greatness and remarkable personal attributes.

One does not bend history by being the lesser of two evils.

GRABBING POWER FOR POWER'S SAKE

For years, conservatives made themselves feel better about their permanent minority status in Washington by justifying their abject failure at congressional politics. One popular argument among the conservative smart set was that the GOP's continued failure to control Congress was a sign of its moral superiority.

That amusing argument went something like this: Democrats were ruthlessly efficient at winning political contests because, as with their descendants in the French Revolution, politics served as their one true religion.

Since these pagan liberals were godless, accumulating power on this earth was their way of compensating for the dreadful burden of knowing that after death, they would spend an eternity separated from God.

The underlying conceit was that for Democrats, the immoral ends always justified the ruthless means.

Republicans, on the other hand, liked to think of themselves as a breed apart. They believed that if ever allowed to run Washington, their party would not sacrifice enduring principles for fleeting power.

Then Republicans took over Washington.

The Republican majority did initially force Bill Clinton to balance the budget, cut taxes, and reform welfare. We also passed the most sweeping congressional reforms in the history of that institution.

But within a few years, Republicanism stopped representing reform and started focusing instead on maintaining the majority. As with the pigs in *Animal Farm,* political definitions were quickly modified to fit the leaders who ran the barn. Soon it became hard to tell the pigs from the humans.

Newt Gingrich called for a government shutdown to force President Clinton to the negotiating table over a balanced budget battle. But when the heat was turned up by Bill Clinton and the media, Speaker Gingrich forced us to shut down the shutdown.

In 1995, Gingrich called our proposed tax cuts the "crown jewels" of the Contract with America.

A few years later, he suggested to the *New York Times* that he could surrender those tax cuts to strike a deal with Mr. Clinton.

It was then that I joined a handful of 1994 classmates who revolted against Gingrich and his lieutenants, who seemed all too eager to fold on critical provisions in the Contract. We refused to allow Newt and his negotiators to bargain away those tax cuts, any more than we would permit backsliding on spending cuts.

We conservatives were once again savaged inside our own Republican Caucus, but we didn't care.

Within days, Gingrich was forced to tell Mr. Clinton that tax cuts were no longer part of the negotiations. The president then consoled the Republican speaker for having to put up with such conservative members.

A few years later when Newt Gingrich gave his last speech as speaker of the House, he chose the occasion to mock us as the "perfectionist caucus."

Once again, Mr. Gingrich chose to side with the liberal likes of Wisconsin Democrat David Obey instead of the conservatives whose election had made him speaker.

The "perfectionist caucus's" crime was refusing to go along with the speaker and Democratic appropriations who passed what was then the most bloated omnibus appropriators bill in years.

For Newt Gingrich and his allies, the conservatives who were swept into Congress in 1994 had seemed, at times, to be more trouble than they were worth.

Soon he would find himself siding with Bill Clinton in budget negotiations and apologizing to the Democratic president for not being able to better control his young, radical freshmen.

But the only thing radical about Joe Scarborough, Mark Sanford, Tom Coburn, Steve Largent, and Matt Salmon was that we wanted to keep the promises we made in our campaigns.

The day after the 1998 elections, a small group of conservatives called the speaker to tell him he would not be reelected to run the House. By the time Matt Salmon appeared on *Larry King Live* to tell the CNN host he had the votes required to dispose of Gingrich, the political world knew his reign was over.

Karl Rove would later say that Newt Gingrich had become such a political liability that George W. Bush would never have been elected president if Gingrich had still been speaker.

That sentiment is shared today by many GOP candidates, who believe their losses over the past four years were the result of Mr. Bush's unpopularity.

WAG THE DOGMA

Unfortunately, once Newt Gingrich left town, things would soon go from bad to worse.

Within months of President Bush's first inauguration, GOP leaders on the Hill started acting like their "pagan" enemies in the Democratic Party. Republican leaders had underestimated their own ability to be brutally efficient in adjusting to the new realities of power. In fact, they proved to be terribly nimble when it came to promoting party power over personal principle.

Soon enough, being "conservative" became synonymous with supporting President Bush, and those who opposed the president's leftward lurches in education, spending, and entitlement programs were blasted for aiding and abetting the radical Left.

Whatever George W. Bush decided was conservative was immediately defined in Republican circles as "conservative."

It was the ideological equivalent of Richard Nixon telling David Frost that the law was what Richard Nixon said it was, because he was, after all, the president.

Unfortunately, this mindless descent into Republicanism didn't stop with politics.

Several of my conservative friends who worked in churches told stories of how their members would challenge others in the congregation if they did not fully support George W. Bush's political agenda. Some churchgoers began believing that one could not be a good Christian without blindly supporting Mr. Bush.

It was all too much for my evangelical friends, who actually had to sit down and explain to their parishioners that while they had also voted for President Bush, his political platform was not inspired by Jesus Christ.

Democrats would also complain after 9/11 of having their patriotism impugned if they did not fall in line with the White House's war plans. While much of that was political posturing by the Left, there is no doubt that some of the president's men tried to link patriotism with strict adherence to Mr. Bush's policies.

But Democrats were not the only ones whose love of country was questioned.

Perhaps the most offensive form of Republicanism that I witnessed during the Bush era came in the form of a *National Review* cover story that accused conservatives who opposed Bush's Iraq policy of hating America.

National Review contributing editor and former Bush speechwriter David Frum said of war dissenters like Pat Buchanan and Robert Novak, "They are thinking about defeat, and wishing for it, and they will take pleasure in it if it should happen. They began by hating the neoconservatives. They came to hate their party and this president. They have finished by hating their country."

It is hard reading that *National Review* piece years later and not being struck by a sense of sadness that the Bush apologists who hijacked the conservative movement over the past decade sank to such low rhetorical levels. After all, *National Review* founder William Buckley had concluded himself that George Bush was not a conservative.

How ironic that the political movement that Russell Kirk described in *The Conservative Mind* as rejecting dogma and ideology would become so infected by the rigidity of Republicanism.

And how ironic that such attacks would emanate from publications like the *National Review*, since the founder of that invaluable publication himself said the U.S. enterprise in Iraq was "anything but conservative."

"Conservatism," Buckley told *Wall Street Journal* editorial writer Joe Rago in 2005, "except when it is expressed as pure idealism, takes into account reality, and the reality of the situation is that missions abroad to effect regime change in countries without a bill of rights or democratic tradition are terribly arduous. This isn't to say that the war is wrong, or that history will judge it to be wrong. But it is absolutely to say that conservatism implies a certain submission to reality; and this war has an unrealistic basis and is being conscripted by events."

One wonders what Mr. Frum and his fellow neoconservatives whispered about Bill Buckley behind his back in the final years of his fascinating life.

I should explain what many readers may already know.

I work with Pat Buchanan almost daily and find him to be one of the most gracious, patriotic Americans I have ever met. Though I am far more optimistic than he is about the future of our great land, I have met no one in Congress or in the media who loves their country any more than Ronald Reagan's former communications director.

I have also been an admirer of David Frum from afar.

I eagerly read *Dead Right* after moving to Washington in 1994 and also supported the Iraq War.

Unlike many, I was cheered by his words that properly identified Iraq, Iran, and North Korea as the "Axis of Evil." But I was, and remain, offended by the suggestion that conservative stalwarts like Pat Buchanan and Robert Novak were guilty of hating America because they did not support Mr. Bush's efforts to move us into a war that Bill Buckley himself said was no more conservative an enterprise than the president who launched it.

That is the sort of dogmatic thinking that had its origins in the French Revolution, and it is a brand of politics that all conservatives, including myself, must abandon.

The *National Review* attack was more than a personal insult delivered to Buchanan and Novak. It was a harsh, dogmatic approach to politics that infected far too many Republicans over the past eight years. The ideological rigidity of Republicanism seems more in line with the type of liberal radicalism that was anathema to founders of conservatism like Edmund Burke and Russell Kirk.

It has been a bizarre sight to see Republican apparatchiks defining conservatism by what positions George Bush decided to take on any given day.

I suppose that it's typical in Washington, but the conservative movement's descent into personality-cult politics strapped Republicans with Wilsonian worldviews and something that began being described as "big-government conservatism."

Big-government conservatism?

Woodrow Wilson Republicans?

Really?

Is it any wonder that the Republican Party got slaughtered at the ballot box over the last two elections?

ABSOLUTE POWER MAKES ABSOLUTE IDIOTS

Republicans should just admit that America turned its government over to the GOP and we blew it. We Republicans forgot why we were elected, and more important, we forgot why we got into public service in the first place.

Lord Acton's much-quoted insight on power applies too perfectly to leave out of this chapter. Power does corrupt, and absolute power corrupts absolutely.

It happened to Roman emperors as it did to medieval popes; it brought down French monarchs and it infected conservatives who ran Washington, D.C., at the beginning of the twenty-first century.

On the cold January day in 2005 when George W. Bush delivered his second inaugural address, the president surveyed what should have been a conservative landscape. A Republican president was beginning his second term with a similarly reelected Republican House and Senate for the first time since 1928.

Unfortunately, the corrosive effects of four years of Republicanism would haunt his second term.

The mistakes of Iraq that no conservative dared correct in the early days of that war would blow up in a spectacular way.

The GOP's refusal to refrain from reckless spending policies would lead to massive debts and a weakened economy.

And the culture of Republicanism that bred a culture of fear around the president meant there would be no aide in the West Wing who could tell the president to stop looking at Katrina's devastation from 40,000 feet and instead get his damn boots on the ground.

Republicans spent Mr. Bush's first term working feverishly to consolidate political power instead of building a conservative agenda. Many of my friends who were the idealists who stormed the imperial Congress in 1994 became cynical congressmen who had mastered the ways of Washington.

One conservative who had spent more than a few meetings getting pummeled inside Newt Gingrich's office now seemed contemptuous of my lecturing on the need for smaller government. As I complained about Republicans' reckless ways, I asked what had happened to all the reformers who came to Congress to change Washington.

He offered a mocking laugh and said, "We grew up, Scarborough."

This Republican who was once considered a conservative stalwart then tried to get under my skin by reeling off all the pork-barrel projects he had secured for his district.

I poked back by telling him that he should be more like another conservative from his home state who was rejecting those earmarks.

"Why should I? He will lose next year and I won't."

Sadly, he was right. It was another victory for Republicanism that was repeated countless times during the Bush era.

In 1994, Republican candidates like my formerly conservative friend ran as Washington outsiders who promised to balance the budget, pay off the federal debt, and change the way Congress spent taxpayers' money. We promised Americans that if we got elected, we would be different.

But over time, Washington changed all but the strongest of conservatives.

The reform impulse that won the House in 1994 was forgotten by the time George W. Bush was sworn in. Reform was replaced by self-dealing and incumbent protection plans.

The earmarking epidemic was directly responsible for the parade of GOP scandals that ensnarled lobbyist Jack Abramoff, Tom Delay, his GOP staffers Tony Rudy and Michael Scanlon, and congressmen Duke Cunningham and Bob Ney.

THE ERA OF BIG GOVERNMENT HAS RETURNED

Republicans have fallen far from the days of Ronald Reagan's "Government is not the solution to our problem; government is the problem" to George Bush's "We have a responsibility that when somebody hurts, government has got to move."

Ronald Reagan believed government needed to stay out of America's way. George W. Bush believed it needed to play a more central role in Americans' lives.

What else would explain the fact that federal spending rose faster under George Bush than under any president since Lyndon Johnson?

In Mr. Bush's first year, the government devoured "only" 18.5 percent of our economy. That was the most efficient government since 1969. In fact, federal spending was a lower percentage of the gross domestic product than it was during the Reagan years, when the federal government tore through 22 percent of the economy in Mr. Reagan's efforts to destroy the Soviet Empire.

Those percentages remained high through George H. W. Bush's presidency and the early years of Bill Clinton's reign. In 1992, Washington spending stood at 22.1 percent of GDP. But three years after the conservative revolution of 1994, that rate had dropped 3 percentage points, to 19.2 percent. Because conservatives were forcing the federal government to live within its means, Bill Clinton reluctantly told America during his 1996 state of the union address that "the era of big government is over."

Once George W. Bush moved into the White House, the great conservative advancements of the 1990s abruptly came to an end. Mr. Bush simply refused to say "no" to the old GOP bulls.

Over his first term in office, the deficit and national debt soared to record levels but Mr. Bush never once lifted his veto pen. By refusing to cross his political allies, the president put Republicanism ahead of conservative values. The result, again, was disastrous.

Congressional members made matters worse by returning the president's favor in refusing to apply any restraint to the White House's own massive spending programs. The same Republican Congress that was willing to shut down the federal government to balance the budget was now afraid to pick up the phone to tell the president he was endangering the future of the U.S. economy.

Because they didn't, appropriations chairmen built bridges to nowhere, bureaucratic administrators' departments swelled, politicians of all stripes got reelected, and the taxpayer got left holding the bill.

By 2007, the government was spending over $2,700,000,000,000.00 in a single year. To put that in perspective, Mr. Bush's year-by-year budget grew by more than $1,000,000,000,000.00 in a single presidency. That massive growth of the centralized state was unprecedented in American history. It also accounted for 22 percent of America's GDP.

Republicans had asked the voters to give them free rein in Washington and they got their wish. The result was great for Republicanism but terrible for America. It also destroyed the conservative movement for a time.

That collapse in turn led to the election of a left-wing president and Congress who passed an annual budget that was $3,500,000,000,000.00 instead of $2,700,000,000,000.00.

President Bush's "big-government Republicanism" applied to regulations as well as spending.

In a recent paper, economists Veronique de Rugy and Melinda Warren measured what they called the federal agencies' "incredible growth" in regulatory reach.

When George Bush entered the White House in 2000, the government spent $21 billion merely on the bureaucracies that administer the government's social regulations, and $4.3 billion was spent on economic regulation, up from respectively $11 billion and $2.5 billion at the end of the Reagan era.

But by 2008, social regulation costs had nearly doubled, to $41 billion, and economic regulation had shot up almost 75 percent, to $7 billion.

That means that George W. Bush's presidency saw regulation costs skyrocket by a shocking 65 percent. By contrast, Bill Clinton's jumped by only 8 percent in his first term, and 21 percent in his second.

Imagine if Bill Clinton had allowed regulation to grow at such a rapid rate. The reaction would have been deafening from all conservative corners.

We would have also savaged Mr. Clinton politically had he taken a $155 billion surplus and turned it into a trillion-dollar debt. But for some reason, conservatives remained mute as government spending and regulations shot up at crippling rates.

The party of less spending and less regulation suddenly became the party of bigger deficits, bloated budgets, and runaway regulation.

Mr. Bush became the first Republican president since Dwight Eisenhower to run for that office without calling for or abolishing a single government program. More troubling than that was the fact that the agencies that Republicans had tried to abolish in the 1994 revolution grew at faster rates under the Bush White House than under any other administration in history.

Bigger government, crippling debts, bloated bureaucracies, military adventurism, incompetent governance, and ideological stridency were just a few of the hallmarks of Republicanism as practiced in the Age of Bush.

The question we should be asking ourselves today is not why conservatives did so little to address these disasters. Rather, it is, why did the Republican Party do so many things that actively made each one of these crises worse?

The answer is, in a word, Republicanism.

We have to do better, and we will. And we must begin our journey back to power by remembering Ronald Reagan's greatest lesson.

9 THE GIPPER'S GREATEST LESSON

BRINGING GRACE TO A BLOOD SPORT

All legislation, all government, all society is founded upon
the principle of mutual concession, politeness, comity,
courtesy; upon these everything is based . . . Let him who
elevates himself above humanity, above its weaknesses, its
infirmities, its wants, its necessities, say, if he pleases, I will
never compromise; but let no one who is not above the
frailties of our common nature disdain compromises.

—*Henry Clay*

You can catch more flies with honey.

—*Mom*

The news wasn't good for Ronald Reagan that morning. The retired president was raked over the coals that day by the *L.A. Times*
and editorial enemies who had loathed the conservative icon from
his days as California governor.

The *Times* exacted more than a pound of flesh from Mr. Reagan in that edition, attacking him for everything from his role in the Iran-Contra scandal to his complicity in the nation's exploding deficit crisis.

As a biographer of the former president slipped into the back-seat of a car to be driven to the Reagans' home, he took a quick look at the front page of the *Times* and groaned. The old man would be in no mood to talk today.

When he arrived at the Reagans' new home in Bel Air, Nancy met him at the front door with a scowl. The protective wife was understandably upset by the day's news, and as Reagan's biographer, Edmund Morris, was shown to the back patio, he wondered whether he should just ask the president if there would be a better day to reflect on his years in the White House.

Walking onto the sunlit back porch, Morris saw the 40th president of the United States glowering at the front page of the *L.A. Times*.

"Good morning, Mr. President," Morris said cheerfully.

But Reagan would have nothing to do with niceties on this day.

"Have you seen the paper?" Reagan asked with a rage barely contained.

"Yes, Mr. President, I have. I'm so sorry. I was wondering . . ."

But Reagan cut him off, while folding the paper in half and throwing it across the breakfast table toward his biographer.

A red-faced Reagan then leaned across the table and pointed to an article on the lower left side of the front page, hidden well below the stories bashing Morris's subject.

Reagan narrowed his eyes and then said with disgust, "I can't believe the O'Malleys are even thinking about selling the Dodgers to Murdoch."

His biographer took a quick look at the baseball story and let out a laugh. The moment was quintessentially Reagan.

Even after eight grueling years in the White House, the political legend was still a man who was so secure in his beliefs that he rarely kept score on opponents who launched hateful attacks against him.

Ronald Reagan never wasted his political audience's time in vicious screeds against opponents or with intemperate remarks meant to destroy those who opposed him.

His positive approach was a winning strategy that another politician and president from California would have done well to emulate, instead of keeping enemies lists and trying to destroy political opponents. But Richard Nixon's paranoia and vengefulness stood in stark contrast to the Gipper's temperament.

Reagan refused to turn political opponents into punching bags. Instead, he would try to make them his friends.

CBS News legend Lesley Stahl told *Morning Joe* of how she would interview various groups during the Reagan administration before they entered the White House. More often than not, Stahl remembers those delegations walking in angry and telling reporters how they were planning to give Reagan a piece of their minds.

But as Stahl recalled those West Wing get-togethers 25 years later, she broke out into a wide smile recounting how most of those showdowns ended.

"The delegations would walk outside after meeting the president and be reduced to jelly. Even his toughest opponents were no match for Reagan's charm," Stahl recalled.

Whether Reagan gained his inspiration from Jesus Christ, who instructed his followers to turn the other cheek, or from Michael Corleone, who advised his mob bosses to keep their enemies closest, Ronald Reagan knew how to win people over.

The Gipper's political results were unrivaled by any conservative before or since he commanded center stage in American politics.

While president, Ronald Reagan would spend his days fighting

U.S. House speaker Tip O'Neill's Democratic majority. The two leaders engaged in fierce battles over nothing less than the future direction of American government.

The stakes could not have been higher. But while many of the two leaders' subordinates would make intemperate remarks about Reagan's White House or O'Neill's House members, both men would look forward to evenings when the two Irishmen could get together to drink whiskey, tell stories, and laugh at each other's jokes.

Think of how far we have traveled from that place in America's recent history where two political giants could hold extremely different political views but approach every battle with the belief that each only wanted the best for his country. They also seemed to understand that it was in the republic's best interest to have a vibrant debate where personal animus didn't get in the way of America's future.

I am not suggesting that these two men didn't grumble about their political adversaries or engage in hardball tactics to get their way. Both did.

But they always kept their battles in the proper perspective and believed that as Americans they had more issues that united them than separated them.

Ronald Reagan's relationship with the liberal speaker underlined the fact that he was conservative ideologically but moderate temperamentally.

The dichotomy between Reagan the politician and Reagan the person is what made him the one conservative national leader that even liberals found hard to hate. His ability to neutralize political opponents with goodwill and charm was one of Reagan's most effective political weapons. He used it frequently and with ruthless efficiency.

I often wonder why conservatives who are so quick to hold

Ronald Reagan up as a model for leadership celebrate his right-wing ideology but forget about the man's "winning smile."

Pat Buchanan ran President Reagan's White House communications shop and remembers Reagan as a man incapable of holding grudges or keeping score. He also remembers that the man who first gained the widespread support of Christian fundamentalists always kept an open-minded attitude toward friends and colleagues. He was more Californian than Pentacostal.

Reagan took people as they were and left the spiritual judgments to God. I wish I could say the same about the politicians who rule Washington today.

I remember walking onto the floor of Congress for the first time after my election. As I entered through the chamber's front doors, I saw Republicans swirling around the right side of the chamber while Democrats stuck with their types on the other side.

After a few days, I noticed that the two sides rarely mingled. The aisle that the president marches down to make his state of the union address one night a year was used for the other 364 days as an official line of demarcation between rival parties that behaved more like angry street gangs.

The only thing missing on Congress's center aisle was a Checkpoint Charlie complete with barbed wire and guard dogs. After a few weeks I had had enough. I crossed the dividing line and started talking to any Democrat who would make eye contact.

Over time, I began seeking out the most liberal members in the chamber to try to understand how two representatives in the same institution could have such diametrically opposed views.

One of the most instructive conversations I had in the first year in Congress was with California representative Ron Dellums. The liberal congressman had long been loathed by conservatives outside of Washington as the type of 1960s radical who had ruined America.

I wanted to meet this man that so many of my ideological brethren feared. To my surprise, Dellums was eager to talk to a young, conservative Republican. But before I could ask my first question, the aging liberal icon beat me to the punch.

"There's one thing I can't figure out," Dellums began. "Why is it that all you cats around here with the energy are conservative? Back in my day you would have been on my side!"

I thought about it for a minute and then answered.

"When you think about Republicans, you associate us with Vietnam, Watergate, and segregation. When I think about Democrats, I associate you with Iranian hostages, 20 percent interest rates, and malaise."

Ron looked at me and then let out a loud laugh.

He talked for the next several minutes about how he had gotten into politics, and did so with warmth and grace. Before leaving he said, "I like you, Scarborough. We have to do this again."

We did. And I learned many more insights about my country by talking to someone with whom I disagreed than I would have if I had remained on my side of that divided chamber.

Over the next few years, I spent time building friendships with other liberals who were ideological opposites of a conservative Baptist from the panhandle of Florida. One of the more interesting relationships I developed was with Maxine Waters.

Like Ron Dellums, Maxine was considered one of the more liberal members. She certainly played to that left-wing typecasting in one memorable Judiciary hearing, where she suggested that all Republicans supporting a certain piece of legislation before the committee were racist.

It was too much for me to take.

"Mr. Chairman," I said in Henry Hyde's direction while interrupting Waters midsentence, "could I raise a point of personal privilege?"

Chairman Hyde obliged but didn't look pleased that I was about to turn his hearing into a debate over racial politics. But that's exactly what I did.

I spent the next few minutes asking Congresswoman Waters exactly whom she considered to be a bigot on the Republican side of the committee room. The exchange soon became heated, but it was broken up by a vote on the floor.

As committee members scattered for the upcoming vote, Henry Hyde walked past with a smile and said, "Don't encourage her, Mr. Scarborough. Just leave it alone."

But I couldn't.

I walked over to the Los Angeles liberal and began talking to her. Maxine collected her papers and started walking toward the House floor. For the next 10 minutes we exchanged tough words that neither heard, but I kept following her. When we got to the House floor to vote, she finally turned to me and her stern face dissolved into a smile.

"You know what, Joe? You're crazy! Leave me alone!" Maxine turned around and walked off.

I spent the next few months seeking out the congresswoman on the House floor. I would make her nervous by hugging her in front of cameras during important votes.

"Stop, Scarborough! Stop! You're going to cost me votes in my district!" Maxine would shout out in mock horror. She would then return the favor during votes where conservatives would be more likely to be watching.

Ten years later, when I come back to the House floor there are few members of Congress I enjoy seeing more than Maxine Waters. The fact that our friendship began in a heated exchange makes that relationship more special.

That is not to say that we agree on virtually anything, whether the debate involves the support of Fannie Mae or Barack Obama's exorbitant spending plans. But we still disagree on the key issues of the day without attacking each other personally.

Of course, my days in Congress were not filled completely with sweetness and light. My first few years in the House were often consumed with anger toward the Clinton administration and those who I believed were standing in the way of a balanced budget, a smaller federal government, and a reformed welfare system.

Policy battles during the Contract with America were particularly nasty.

Democrats regularly accused Republicans of wanting to starve children, abandon seniors, and take from the poor to reward the rich. Civil rights legend John Lewis, whom I also consider a good friend, even compared my friends and me to Birmingham's notorious Democratic police chief Bull Connor.

What did we do to draw comparisons from Lewis with a man who had let dogs loose on peaceful civil rights protesters? Well, we had supported increasing funding for school lunch programs by 4 percent instead of 6 percent. For that crime, we were compared to thuggish segregationists and accused of wanting to take food from the mouths of babes.

As would have been the case with most people in my position, I flinched when I heard John's speech. But I didn't dissolve into anger as I would have in earlier days. Instead, I went up to him after his hyperbolic speech and politely expressed my concerns before we walked back to our offices together.

My friendship with John remains to this day. But it requires us both to overlook strong words and personal slights that inevitably come along in this business. Even as I write this, I am sure that John and Maxine could present a laundry list of votes and speeches I have made that required even greater patience on their part.

Like too many other politicians who are caught up in the day-to-day battles that consume Washington, I often let my temper get the best of me. Too often, I became impatient with those who were not as driven as I was when it came to shrinking the federal government.

As one of the youngest members in Congress, I demanded instant action and ideological purity from those on both sides of the aisle. What a shame that youth is wasted on the young.

Often, the targets of my outbursts were moderate Republicans whose political lives did not begin the day I walked through the chamber's doors. But more often than not, Bill Clinton was the object of many wrathful interviews and congressional speeches I wish I could now take back.

I don't regret those actions because I have grown to appreciate the former president's policy positions. Nor is it because I now better understand all the president's personal motivations. But rather it is because striking out at Mr. Clinton in anger was bad for me personally and for the Republican Party in general.

Let me crack the code for fellow conservatives who still believe that showing kindness and grace to people not in our party is a bad thing.

American elections are decided every four years by independent and moderate voters who remain disengaged from the political system for as long as humanly possible. They usually begin focusing on congressional elections a few days before the vote and a few weeks before presidential contests are decided.

There is no quicker way to turn these swing voters against you than by appearing angry, combative, and blindly ideological.

These same voters who swung the presidential election for Democrat Barack Obama in 2008 voted twice for Republican George W. Bush, twice for Democrat Bill Clinton, and twice for Republican Ronald Reagan.

They are also the same voters who elected Bill Clinton in 1992, only to turn around two years later and reject the Democratic president for being overly ideological. These same voters then elected Republicans like me in 1994, only to reject us as being too extreme two years later.

Why?

Because the Gingrich Republican Congress was seen as an angry, ideological movement concerned more with advancing rigid dogmas than with solving people's problems. And I suspect young, angry conservatives like myself were, in part, to blame for the re-election of Bill Clinton in 1996.

By taking to the House floor and appearing on cable news shows wearing scowls on our faces, we House Republicans made the Democrat once rejected as extreme look like the voice of moderation and reason. Bill Clinton had learned from his 1994 loss that when it came to swing voters, temperament trumped ideology every time.

My first term in Congress taught me valuable lessons that I carry with me today.

Near the end of 1996, I began watching replays of all my performances on cable news shows. I did not do that because I wanted to, but rather because my staff members forced me to. It seems that while some in my ideological base were thrilled with my angry rants, many more reasonable supporters were growing tired of my temperamental outbursts.

These voters were just as conservative on taxes and spending as anyone else in my district, but they realized that my conservative message was being drowned out by my intense delivery.

As I watched these command performances, my head fell into my hands. On TV, my face would begin turning frightening shades of red. I was horrified at the side of myself that I was showing viewers of political news.

Friends whom I had known for years would ask what had happened to the guy they had played football with or seen perform in a band. The angry, young right-wing tool on TV looked nothing like the Joe they used to know.

I usually dismissed those questions as inquiries from the politically uninitiated. But after watching a few of my sweat-drenched screeds, I felt their pain.

I tried a new strategy. I began to laugh at the preposterousness of Bill Clinton's doublespeak instead of allowing myself to be reduced to rage. Within weeks of my temperamental conversion, staff members started fielding a regular stream of calls from news programs that wanted me on their shows.

I was soon getting the better of most of my political opponents by smiling while they were shouting. And where they started spitting out talking points, I began telling jokes about the sillier parts of their agenda.

Weeks later, my staff sat me down again to view my latest round of interviews. It took just a few seconds of watching to notice a dramatic change. I saw for myself that the conservative message I wanted to get through to Americans was no longer being held hostage by right-wing rage.

I had not become more moderate in my political views. I had just become more accessible in my temperament.

That was a lesson I would try to apply throughout the rest of my congressional career. And while I remained one of the most conservative members of Congress when it came to fighting for limited government, I tried my best to remain moderate enough in my public persona so as not to scare small children or household pets.

I remained a fixture on cable news and shows like *Politically Incorrect*. I also received positive press coverage from reporters at newspapers like the *New York Times* and the *Washington Post* despite the fact that my political views were far more conservative than those of the people who covered me.

Fellow conservative classmates began asking how I received such positive reviews when so many other Republicans in Congress got skewered by national outlets. I told them it was simple. Unlike many who were elected in that 1994 class, I didn't consider the media to be my sworn enemy. In fact, I usually enjoyed walking off the House floor and talking with the young reporters who covered Congress more than I did chatting with fellow congressmen.

I gave my friends simple advice when it came to relations with the press: "Even your dog knows when you hate him. It might help if the next time you walk through the press gallery, you show a little less contempt for the people who cover you."

For some reason, many of my fellow conservatives never figured that out.

I would like to be able to say that the hard lessons learned in Congress remained with me when I became a member of the press myself. But that wasn't the case.

In 2003, MSNBC hired me as a commentator on the network. Though they never said as much, I think the reason was that they wanted to be more balanced in their coverage of the coming war in Iraq. Of all the political talk hosts who were employed by the network, I would be the only one who supported the war.

In those early days at the network, taking that position was extremely unpopular with NBC employees. I was seen as a right-wing interloper and a commentator who would be a better fit at Fox News than at the network where I now worked.

Perhaps it was the scorn that I felt being heaped upon me every day at work, or maybe I was tired of hearing the same liberals who had attacked Ronald Reagan for standing firm against the Soviet Union now attacking the new Republican president for challenging Saddam Hussein.

Or just maybe it was the fact that I had executives (who are no longer employed by MSNBC) demanding that I attack my liberal guests without mercy.

Whatever the reason, those first few months on TV were terrible. Not only did I allow myself to be put in a position where I was forced to ignore every lesson I had learned in Congress, I was also being criticized by top executives at NBC for not being harsh enough on my program.

"I need more, Joe. Give me more!" came the pleas from 30 Rock.

Perhaps my bosses had been set off by an interview with Fox

News impresario Roger Ailes, who had predicted my demise inside the pages of the *New York Observer* for not being confrontational enough.

Despite the fact that I considered Roger's words to be an unintended compliment, my bosses at MSNBC and NBC did not.

But their criticisms soon fell on deaf ears.

I decided that I would rather be practicing law in Pensacola than working on a news show that went against every instinct I had. Shouting and snarling were not in Reagan's political playbook, and I didn't want them in mine.

I finally went to the office of my friend Phil Griffin and asked him to intervene with network executives.

"Phil," I said in exasperation, "I can't be shocked, stunned, and enraged five segments a night, five nights a week. That's just not who I am."

Phil took my concerns to his bosses, who finally decided that the role of an angry right-wing talk-show host was not a tight fit for a guy who counted Maxine Waters and John Lewis as his friends. With the 2004 election beginning in a few months, I would be able to play the role of political analyst more than polemical political pundit.

That news was well received by my wife, Susan.

During the first six months of my TV career, I would arrive at my back door after finishing a taping only to find Susan standing inside the door with her arms crossed. She would shoot me a disgusted look, shake her head, and go to bed.

One night before turning her back to me, she gave me some pointed advice.

"Stop being something you're not. Try to be more like Tim Russert," she said.

"Honey," I replied, "they already have one of those."

"Well, they need another Russert more than they need an idiot performing a political vaudeville act every night."

I may have played an idiot on TV, but I was smart enough to let

Susan have the last word that night. I smiled after her searing review, because I knew she was right.

Over the next several years, I took her advice to heart.

While I still criticized the Democratic Party for their excesses, I also went after Republicans when they came up short on the budget, the war, and Hurricane Katrina.

After Don Imus left the network in 2007, I asked Phil to give me a chance to replace the broadcasting legend. Since he was now the president of MSNBC, Phil was again in a position to help. But his offer of assistance came with a strong piece of advice.

"I'll let you try it, Joe," Griffin said. "But you have to remember that you have an audience of one. And his name is Tim Russert."

That was great news, since Tim had always been the newsman I had admired most. It was also great that I could obey my boss at work while telling my wife that she had been right all along.

"Honey, you know that thing you told me about Russert? Well, I've been thinking about what you said and . . ."

My days as an angry cable news host were behind me, and I would be rewarded greatly for following my instincts in the years to come.

What a difference a smile makes.

Whether in politics or the news media, conservatives need to begin following Ronald Reagan's example. No president since Herbert Hoover was as conservative as President Reagan. He was a leader who feared no media boss or Washington power broker despite the fact that most in those elite circles had long considered him a joke.

Reagan never struck back at his enemies or felt the need to justify himself. He would take the slings and arrows with a smile and always appeared to Americans as the most centered man in Washington.

You can rest assured knowing that President Reagan would have never called Barack Obama a Communist. Nor would he have questioned the patriotism or motives of his political opponents.

Those may be shrewd strategies for selling books or driving up TV ratings, but they are not the way to build a winning conservative majority.

While confronting a president who is deeply unpopular with the conservative base is great for ratings, it is a task that must be handled with the greatest of care by conservative leaders who hope to replace that popular leader in the next four years.

The conservative movement must face up to the fact that the same tactics that inspire the base and bring some young ideological voters to the party often come with a political price.

So the question is, how do conservatives keep their base energized without alienating swing voters?

The first necessary step is to stay true to conservative values.

Too often, politicians who target swing voters mistakenly toss out their most important values. That is a terrible mistake. I have found that given the opportunity to vote for a real Democrat or a Republican imitating a Democrat, Americans will vote for the real Democrat every time.

Moderating on conservative principles for the sole sake of attracting moderate voters is always the pathway to defeat for a conservative.

Think about it. Every time the Republican Party elects a moderate presidential nominee, the party loses.

John McCain didn't have any better luck getting elected than did Gerald Ford, Bob Dole, or George H. W. Bush.

Moderating your political platform may win passing praise from liberal reporters, but it will turn off your base and fail ultimately to sway *any* member of the *New York Times* editorial board. So hold firm to your convictions.

The second step in winning over swing voters goes to the heart of this chapter's thesis. Conservatives should tear a page out of the

Gipper's playbook by moderating their temperament. If conservatives truly want to win one for the Gipper, they should leave partisan insults and angry invective out of the public debate.

The third step in winning moderate voters is for conservatives to begin following the advice of Jesus and the example of Reagan, by trying more often to turn the other cheek.

I've always been known by family members as my mother's son. I am told I share many of her traits.

But one characteristic that I inherited from my dad is a short memory. As I was growing up, I often heard my mother voicing great frustration at the fact that my father always forgot those who had wronged him. More times than not, she had a good point.

But after getting elected to Congress, I began hearing the same kind of frustrations voiced from my supporters. I simply was not good at carrying political grudges against those who had been less than gracious to my cause.

My first campaign for political office was also my most difficult. Lois Benson was a skilled state legislator and a political professional who wanted to become a member of Congress.

Republicans on the local, state, and national level had placed their bets on Representative Benson and saw me as a risky choice to carry the district for the GOP. When polls late in the campaign showed that I had erased a 40-point deficit to draw within a few points of Ms. Benson, the gloves came off.

I was pounded unmercifully the final week of that campaign on the radio, on TV, and in newspapers. Because I was a young outsider who was seen as a political reformer, I decided to keep my message positive.

I lost several points in polls taken over the last week, but I held on to carry the primary election by 8 points. Still, that election ended with the two campaigns hating each other.

Soon after my victory, a crisis involving military health care hit the front pages of our local newspapers. For the district that was home to more military retirees than any other, that was as important a local issue as any I would face my first few years in Congress.

I wanted to take aggressive action, so I immediately set up an investigative panel to hold a series of town hall meetings while applying pressure to force military leaders to resolve the crisis.

At that time, there were few political positions that would be more important to voters across the region than chair of the TRI-CARE commission. Many civic leaders lobbied to chair that panel, but I instead made a decision that enraged many of my most loyal followers. I appointed Lois.

Like my mother, many of my supporters demanded to know why I would appoint my political enemy to such an important post.

"Because she's not my enemy, and she shouldn't be yours" was my simple reply.

I knew that despite the final ugly stretch of that campaign, Lois was a gifted public servant who would do a good job, while both of us would show the public that two former political enemies could work together for everyone's best interest. It was the right thing to do, but it was also in the best interest of everyone.

On a much grander scale, Barack Obama showed great confidence by appointing Hillary Clinton secretary of state. In so doing, the new president selected a political rival who had suggested months earlier that he did not have the experience to answer a 3 A.M. phone call if that conversation involved an international crisis.

The young president showed similar confidence when he selected Joe Biden as his vice presidential running mate. It was Mr. Biden, after all, who had told Democratic voters a year earlier that the future president was not up to the task of being commander in chief.

Almost 30 years earlier, Ronald Reagan had run a bitter primary campaign against George H. W. Bush. Reagan had to endure months of attacks from a man who dismissed his domestic policies as "voodoo economics" and implied that a Reagan presidency would lead America into war.

Governor Reagan held no grudges, and instead selected Ambassador Bush as his vice president. Reagan also tapped Bush's former campaign manager as his new chief of staff. The choice of James A. Baker III would prove to be one of President Reagan's most inspired personnel decisions.

Ronald Reagan understood better than any politician in the modern era that carrying grudges or showing flashes of anger would get in the way of his conservative message reaching the masses.

While Reagan was the most conservative president in half a century, his moderate personality allowed the Gipper to remain firmly in the mainstream of America's consciousness.

When his opponents seemed angry, Reagan appeared determined.

What came across as ideology in others looked like personal convictions in Ronald Reagan.

And while his political enemies appeared petty, Ronald Reagan showed a patriotic grace.

Historians are still grappling with the complexities of Mr. Reagan's personality. Even those who worked closely with the 40th president for years still do not know whether they ever really got the true measure of the man himself.

But the Ronald Reagan who revealed himself to American voters was always sunny in disposition, measured in tone, and gracious to those with whom he disagreed.

To Ronald Reagan, politics was not a blood sport. It was a patriotic duty.

Conservatives who wish to carry the mantle of Mr. Reagan

would do honor to his memory if they focused as much on his moderate temperament as they did on his conservative philosophy.

Perhaps if they did, conservatives might find, like Ronald Reagan, that showing a little grace may be the surest way to start winning elections again.

About the Author

JOE SCARBOROUGH was elected to Congress in 1994 with 62 percent of the vote, becoming the first Republican to represent northwest Florida since 1873. Joe was reelected three times by landslide margins. In May 2001, Joe retired from Congress. In 2003, he was hired by NBC as a political commentator and host. Scarborough's critically acclaimed book *Rome Wasn't Burnt in a Day* was published in 2004. He can currently be seen on *Morning Joe* with cohost Mika Brzezinski. The three-hour critically acclaimed political show airs weekdays from 6 to 9 A.M. on MSNBC.